NEWARK:
THE BOUNTY OF BEER

BRENDA M. PASK

Joseph Pask

This book is dedicated to my father, Walter Pask and Grandfather, Joseph Pask, who between them gave over sixty years of service to James Hole & Co.'s Castle Brewery in Newark.

D1214127

Walter Pask

Foreword

by Charles Williamson,
Managing Director of William Younger and Company Limited

It is a great honour for William Younger and Company Limited to sponsor this interesting book which chronicles Newark's long and important links with the Brewing Industry.

The business has a long standing presence in Newark, and will continue to develop its commitment to both the town and county operationally and through high profile sponsorships in association with our Brands – particularly Foster's Lager and John Smith's Bitter.

I am certain this book will be of tremendous value to both the professional researcher and enthusiastic amateur with a keen interest in both the town and the Brewing Industry.

Acknowledgements

My thanks are due to Mr George Tattersall-Walker and the staff of John Smith's Tadcaster Brewery archives who supplied information and photographs, Mr Rodney Cousins who made all his brewing research available to me, Mr J. F. Pepper and Mr J. Walker for their memories of the Castle Brewery, Mr Vic Baumber for memories of the Devon Brewery site and Warwicks & Richardson's horses, Mrs Beryl Walker who helped with research, Mr and Mrs N Powers for their memories of Warwicks & Richardson's, Mrs Thelma Aynsley at Newark Town Hall, Mrs Joyce Lawrence who loaned photographs of the Castle Brewery, Michael Jones of the Brewery History Society, The *Newark Advertiser*, Mr Brian W. Heppenstall for the material on the Heppenstall family and the Albion Brewery, and Mr J. Livingston for information on the Newark Temperance Society, Mr Michael Gill who helped with various identifications and background material on the Victoria Brewery, Holdens furniture shop of Newark for the photograph of their renovated shop front, whilst the use of materials from Newark Library, Nottinghamshire Archives and Newark Museum is also gratefully acknowledged.

I am grateful to the following for reading the typescript and for making suggestions and improvements : Rodney Cousins, Michael Honeybone, Peter Stephens, George Tattersall-Walker and Mike Langford of William Younger and Company Limited (East Midlands). Special thanks are due to Ian Brown for his photographic work, and the painstaking hours spent in seeing the book through publication and to Tim Warner, Local Studies Librarian, Newark Library, for his encouragement and help throughout this project.

Contents

1. NEWARK: THE BOUNTY OF BEER

"An old castle in ruins, and a magnificent church, marks the Nottinghamshire town of malt and brewing. Other towns in the county may be more picturesque and more famous for their manufactures, but none can vie with Newark in its malthouses and kilns, or beat the quality of malt manufactured or the beer brewed in that historic Trentside town."

So wrote Alfred Barnard in his 'Noted Breweries of Great Britain and Ireland' of 1889-91. Barnard was inspecting the Newark breweries when the brewing industry was at its height. To understand how Newark came to merit Barnard's accolade, we need to return to the beginning of the brewing story.

The Beginning of Brewing

In ancient times brewing was common in Bible Lands, using malted cereals such as barley. The Ancient Egyptians even had a hieroglyph for "brewer". Early brewing was crude and the necessary techniques of malting and fermentation had probably been discovered by accident. Archaeologists are able to tell us that the earliest brewers would have buried their soaked barley in the ground, to allow it to germinate. It was then dried, crushed and made into large flat cakes which were baked. The cakes were then soaked in warm water and passed through a sieve (a process known as mashing). This would produce a *'wort'* which was fermented in earthenware vessels, using yeast from a previous brew or from fruit on which it occurred naturally. Such beer would be cloudy, and indeed, some was so thick with barley husks that it had to be drunk by means of a hollow reed.

The Romans have often been credited with introducing beer into Britain, but the technique was certainly known long before the invasion and may well have travelled from the Middle East at the same time as barley was introduced.

The Romans did not like the beer they found in Britain. Pliny the Elder wrote contemptuously of the western nations who 'intoxicate themselves by means of moistened grain', and the Emperor Julian's comment on British beer is well known: 'who made you and from what, by the true Bacchus, I know not. He [wine] smells of nectar, but you smell of goat'.

The Romans introduced wine but, although it was adopted by those Britons who became Romanised, the native beer continued to be brewed. (It should more properly be described as 'ale', as it was unhopped beer and continued as such until the 15th Century). There were no breweries as we would recognise them, but brewing was carried out in most people's homes, usually by the women.

With the coming of monasteries, hostels were built to accommodate the large numbers of pilgrims visiting shrines and other holy places. Such hostels became the forerunners of inns, with the monasteries brewing their own ale to provide for visitors. Indeed ale was the only reliable and safe drink available at this time: water and milk, the only alternatives, were too likely to become contaminated and a source of infection. Ale became the staple drink for all - men, women and children.

In Norman times, large quantities of wine were imported but the staple drink remained beer. With a greater degree of political stability in the country, travellers enjoyed more security and roadside inns sprang up to cater for their needs. Such hostelries would brew their own ale.

In the 12th Century, beer was officially recognised as a source of revenue, first of all for local tax collectors and then on a national basis. At the main fairs, ale sold from barrels attracted a toll to be paid to the local Lord of the Manor or the Abbot of the Monastery, and in 1188 Henry II introduced the first national tax on beer to raise money to subsidise the Crusades. This was the so-called 'Saladin Tithe'. Since that time, a tax has been levied on beer until the present day.

In 1267 Henry III fixed the price of beer and bread in his Assize of Bread and Ale. Depending on its strength, ale was fixed at 1d, 1½d and 2d (0.5p, 0.75p, and 1p) per gallon (4.5 litres). Most ale was strong and sweet as it kept better. It was inspected by officials called 'ale conners', who were usually appointed by Local Authorities to test it by drinking. Legend says they had to wear leather breeches when performing their duties, as they were obliged to sit on a drop of ale to test its stickiness.

In the early 15th Century, beer brewed with the use of *hops*, to give added flavour, was imported from the Low Countries. Hops had been used for many years in central Europe to prolong the life of the beer, a function performed in England by making it stronger and sweeter. Now long life could be given to weaker, less sweet, beer.

The new beer at first met with a good deal of resistance. There were fights in London between those who supported ale and those who supported the new hopped beer. Separate guilds were formed to produce the two commodities and they even adopted different sizes of cask for their products. Brewers of hopped beer were probably, at first, viewed with suspicion because they were mainly foreigners.

Now the different beverages could be enjoyed in three different establishments. Hopped beer could be obtained, together with food and board, in inns, and it could also be bought with wine in taverns. Ale was available in the common ale houses but mostly it was brewed and drunk at home.

In the 15th and 16th Centuries, breweries increased in size to meet demand, though most were attached to taverns and ale houses.

In 1495, Henry VII introduced a system of licensing ale houses and in 1577 a census of all taverns, ale houses and inns was taken. The total for England and Wales was 19,759 - one to every 187 people. (It has been calculated that today, the number is about 1 to every 650 people). The reason for the survey was to raise taxes to help pay for the repairing of Dover harbour.

In 1643 beer duty was introduced. 2 shillings (10p) was payable on beer with a pre-duty cost of 6 shillings (30p) per barrel and 6d (2.5p) on that with a cost less than 6 shillings. Tax was also levied on hops. However, Oliver Cromwell, whose father was a brewster, freed the domestic brewer from paying tax.

In 1697, a Malt Tax of nearly a penny per bushel (0.5p per 36 litres) was introduced and by the 19th Century it had reached 4 shillings (20p). It was absorbed by the new Beer Tax in 1880.

In spite of the increase in taxation in the 17th Century, there was a great expansion in the practice of brewing.

One of Newark's earliest inns, the Old White Hart in the Market Place.

Many famous brewing companies were established at this time, including Trumans, Halsey (later Barclay Perkins), Guinness (then Giles Mee) and Calverts. These so-called *'common brewers'* were taking the place of ale house brewers, though much beer continued to be brewed at home.

In the 18th Century, with the increase in population, came a rapid growth in the number and size of breweries. Even so by the middle of the century, the majority of inns and ale houses still brewed their own beer, as did most colleges and hospitals. In 1750, Excise statistics show that 48,421 *victuallers* produced 2,227,200 barrels of strong beer and 1,139,400 barrels of small or table beer, though by 1799 there were fewer than half this number of brewers. From the 1750s, Excise was the single most important source of raising money for the Government, the duty being collected from each district by local Excise Men. Duties on malt, beer and hops rose sharply after the 1790s and there was more reliance on beer supplied by common brewers, especially in the south. Publican brewers were still numerous however in the West, Midlands and North of the country, and as late as 1825, two thirds of the beer brewed in Yorkshire was brewed by *victuallers*.

It was in this second great expansion of the 18th Century that many of today's most famous names in brewing were established: Bass, Worthington, Whitbread, Meux and Charrington.

The 18th Century was also characterised by a parallel development in brewing science and technology. The invention of the steam engine was soon seen as advantageous by the brewer attempting to increase output, allowing many of his operations to be mechanised. The brewer was also assisted by the re-invention in 1780 by Dicas, of the hydrometer which was able to determine accurately the amount of sugar in the *wort*. Another aid was the Fahrenheit thermometer in recording the temperatures so critical in the brewing process.

Another 18th Century contribution to brewing was the widespread adoption of the substance *isinglass*, which continues in use to this day. It is used to clarify beer and shorten the time lapse between brewing and drinking. Isinglass is a semi-transparent substance obtained from the swim bladders of sturgeon.

Most beer and ale in the 18th Century was very strong, and brown or black in colour. The so-called *'small' beer*, which was weaker, was drunk by women and children and was popular at breakfast. The main rival of beer at this time was gin, and in spite of the introduction of the Gin Act in 1736 (which was intended to restrict the number of gin shops), it continued to be popular. Two new developments in beer production, however, ensured that it remained the country's favourite drink - the invention of *porter*, (a mixture of three types of beer producing a thick, strong beverage mainly drunk by the working classes) and East India *Pale Ale*, a sparkling light drink with a pleasant bitter flavour, drunk mainly by the middle and upper classes. In the 19th Century, Burton-on-Trent became the noted capital for the production of Pale Ale in this country, owing to the favourable water conditions found there (see Chapter 2).

In 1840 there were an estimated 50,000 brewers in the country, but by 1880 this number had been halved. The remaining breweries expanded, and to ensure a market for their beer, began to buy public houses. This was the beginning of the 'tied' house system in operation today.

It was during the second half of the 19th Century that organised opposition to beer drinking was at its height. In 1853, all-day Sunday closing was introduced in Scotland, and in Ireland and Wales in 1881. In 1873, the Church of England Temperance Society was established, with the ultimate aim of gaining legislation to ban the public sale of drink, as in individual states in America. As early as 1836, Newark was targeted by temperence agitators when a lecture was given in the town by the energetic temperence agent, Thomas Whittaker. His aim was to encourage his audience to sign the pledge against the 'demon drink', and establish their own temperance societies. In Newark, however - a town already reliant on trade from its maltings and breweries - his reception was not particularly cordial. "The room on my arrival", wrote Whittaker, "was packed with maltsters' and brewers' men . . . several climbed on the backs of the seats . . . and broke them . . . The legs and arms of these flew at my head and . . . the men then danced with delight and jumped 'Jim Crow'. In the scuffle someone managed to pin an old newspaper to my coat-tail and apply a light to it".

It was not until 1877 that the first evidence of a public interest in temperence manifested itself in Newark, when a meeting was held at the Town Hall in February of that year. This large gathering was addressed by the Reverend D. Antcliff of London, and included members of several denominations, especially the Baptist and Methodist churches. Two years later, in June 1879, the Newark Temperance Society was established with Reverend E.B. Shepherd of the Baptist Church as President.

By 1900, Christ Church had its own branch of the Band of Hope (another national abstentionist organisation) with their annual tea recorded in the

The Ossington Coffee Palace (c.1890).

Newark Advertiser for 17th January in that year. Most active of all amongst the prohibitionist section of the temperance movement, however, was the International Order of Good Templars, founded in England by Joseph Malins in 1868. By 1873 they had established three 'lodges' in Newark - named 'Freedom', 'Active' and 'Good Samaritan' - which, together with their Juvenile Temple, could boast a membership of over 370. "The Good Templars of Newark", commented the *Newark Advertiser*, "seem to be making considerable progress and extending their influence on every hand".

Newark's most enduring monument to the rise of Temperance is the Ossington Coffee Palace on Beastmarket Hill. This was given to the town by Charlotte Denison, Viscountess Ossington (of Ossington Hall near Newark), as a memorial to her late husband the first Viscount Ossington, a former Speaker of the House of Commons. It was opened on 16th November 1882 and contained, as well as the coffee room, assembly rooms, a library, billiard room and dormitories for travellers. After the inaugurative luncheon, the Vicar of Newark offered a prayer and the Reverend H.A. Jukes, Vicar of Christ Church, presented an address to the Viscountess on behalf of the Temperance organisations of the town. In December 1883 the Good Templars opened another of their lodges - the "Lady Ossington Lodge" - at the coffee palace, in honour of the good work they saw the building performing in the town. "Lively and encouraging speeches" reported the *Newark Advertiser* "were delivered by Bros. Tyers, Ward, and Gabbatiss, 14 recruits being enrolled under the charter of the new lodge".

Set against the abstentionist fervour of societies such as the Good Templars, it is interesting to note that, churches on the whole were not generally against beer. Across the country there were many instances of Anglican (Church of England) and Methodist owners of breweries who gained a reputation for enlightened management practices, providing their employees with good working conditions and looking after their general welfare, at a time when this was not common. It was only later in the century that Methodist opposition became more evident. It is interesting that in Newark during the 1860s, Joseph Gilstrap, Christopher Heppenstall, Thomas Earp, William Slater, William Moss and Richard Warwick, all owners of breweries, were Church Wardens at the Parish Church.

As the 19th Century drew to a close, it nevertheless became apparent that where the Temperance movements had failed, economic conditions were about to succeed. A prolonged economic depression, together with the advent of the First World War, further reduced an already depleted market for beer. Many famous companies went out of business and after the War, as economic conditions failed to recover, the number of companies continued to decline. Attempts were made to increase demand with new ranges of bottled and canned beers and lagers, but this was only a partial success.

During the inter-War period, two important pieces of legislation were introduced. In 1921, the Licensing Act instituted a system of 'permitted hours' when intoxicants could be sold and consumed: during nine hours in London and eight hours elsewhere with a two hour closure after noon each day. In 1923, meanwhile, the Intoxicating Liquor Act forbade the selling or serving of intoxicants on licensed premises to those under the age of 18, although people over 16 were allowed to buy beer or cider with a meal.

During the Second World War, owing to the scarcity of both raw materials and the finished product, public houses often ran dry. Because of petrol rationing, deliveries of beer were zoned, and the brewers had to swap pubs. In spite of these difficulties, the brewing industry made an important contribution to the maintenance of the nation's morale.

With the coming of peace in 1945, a new era of opportunity was opened up for the brewers and the traditional pub came to take on a new guise. Many have grown in size and diversified to become eating houses, discotheques and meeting places for local societies, as well as

Retirement of Head Cooper and Barrel Yard Foreman, Mr Walter Trickett (centre) after 48 years service at Hole's Brewery, 30th April 1968.

the purveyors of alcoholic liquor. The process of brewing, meanwhile, has become vested in the hands of fewer and fewer companies, following numerous mergers and take-overs. The selling and consumption of beer has greatly expanded, being freed still further in the 1990s by more relaxation in the licensing laws.

2. THE RAW MATERIALS

Beer today is made from only five main ingredients - water, malt, hops, yeast and sugar.

Water

The quality and type of water is most important in brewing. It is said that it takes 5-7 pints of water (approximately 3-4 litres) to produce one pint (approximately 0.5 litre) of beer. Most of it is needed for heating, cooling and washing. To produce *pale ales*, the water must not only be uncontaminated but also high in gypsum (calcium sulphate) as at Burton-on-Trent. Nowadays, such water can be produced by a process called *'Burtonisation'*, but in the 19th Century breweries were dependent upon what was naturally available. Fortunately, Newark lies in a similar geological formation to Burton and this undoubtedly encouraged the development of the brewing industry in the town (an extensive gypsum industry was already established in the Beacon Hill area and has continued through the 19th and 20th Centuries).

Both the large breweries in Newark were situated where suitable water was readily obtainable. Warwicks & Richardson's on Northgate had a well 90ft (27 metres) deep, supplying water for cooling and washing, pumped up to the great cistern at 15,000 gallons (68,000 litres) per hour. For brewing however, water was pumped from springs on Beacon Hill, where the company had its own pumping station.

Malt workers at James Hole & Co.'s Trentside maltings in the 1880s.
The central figure standing with bare feet is thought to be Charles Smith of Water Lane.

Caparn and Hankey's Brewery, on Albert Street, later taken over by James Hole & Co., took advantage of the same excellent water source used by a starch factory which had preceded them on the site. Indeed the quality of ground water in the region of Albert Street was regarded as sufficient to justify building a new enlarged brewery on that site, rather than in a more convenient location with access to the company's Trentside maltings and rail and river transport.

Eventually, James Hole & Co. decided to sink a new well to take advantage of water with a similar mineral content to that from which Burton Pale Ales were brewed. In spite of encountering many practical difficulties during the boring process, the faith of the brewers was finally justified and water, rich in gypsum, was discovered 894 feet below the surface. Mr. F. Short as foreman of the Barrel Yard, held a barrel to receive the first flow.

Malt

Malt is simply barley which has been allowed to sprout before being 'cured' or heated. Only the best barley is suitable for malting and the area around Grantham was renowned for its production. Indeed James Hole, owner of one of Newark's largest breweries, preferred it to all others. Germination frees the starch in the grain and transforms some of it into sugar. The 'curing' or kilning halts germination and dries the malt, and the degree of heat determines the colour of the resulting brew. The hotter it is, the darker the colour (65°- 80°C for lagers, 85°-100°C for ales and stouts). Although the process sounds simple, it is actually very complex, for malt easily deteriorates. When the brewery has received the malt from the maltster, it has to be kept perfectly dry at a temperature of 60°C in a special malt store until it is needed for brewing. (A full account of the malting process is to be found in Peter Stephens' book 'Newark, the Magic of Malt' pp 15-20 - see Bibliography).

Hops

As described in Chapter 1, old English 'beer' or 'ale' was un-hopped, indeed the use of hops once being regarded as an adulteration of the beer. Now however, hops are regarded as a most important ingredient, giving flavour to the beer. They are especially important in the manufacture of *'bitter'* and *'light'* ales. Hops also preserve the beers from deterioration after brewing. Traditionally hops are grown in Kent, Worcestershire, Herefordshire and Sussex, although today they tend to be imported from Germany, U.S.A. and China.

The hop is a climbing vine-like plant grown on a network of wires seven

The Hop Store at James Hole & Co.'s brewery, c.1935.

metres high, producing its seeds in a cluster or 'cone'. Today new varieties, growing only 2 metres high, have made harvesting easier. The cones are harvested in the autumn and dried in oast houses with their characteristic pointed roof cowls. Hops can be used in the cone or in a powder, pellet or extract form. After use, the 'spent hops' are sold for fertiliser.

Yeast

Yeast is a microscopic fungus. The type used in brewing is bred specially for the job and different strains give different types of beer their characteristic flavour. Yeast has to be treated with great care. If it is too hot or too cold, or its conditions too acid or too alkaline, yeast cannot ferment properly.

An individual yeast cell is invisible to the naked eye but a colony, for example on fruit such as grapes or plums, can be seen as a fine powdery film. Yeast feeds on sugars, converting them into energy to grow and multiply. Because of its ability to renew itself, brewers produce tons more than they need, the excess being sold on to other producers of foodstuffs, notably for use in health food products. Great care has to be taken to prevent the brewing yeast becoming contaminated with different kinds of airborne 'wild' yeast which can interbreed with disastrous consequences for the brew. To prevent this, the yeast cellar at a brewery must be kept carefully sterilised, its air filtered and conditioned, and its temperature maintained between 5°C and 10°C. In James Hole's brewery on Newark's Albert Street, yeast was stored in slate vessels in a white tiled cellar.

3. THE PROCESS OF BREWING

Before it can be used for brewing, the crisp, dark *malt* with a sweet, toffee-like flavour, must be cleansed of all dust and foreign bodies (such as stones, peas, beans etc), which may have come in from the harvest fields. First it is run down a chute containing powerful magnets to remove any metal fragments, as a spark from these could ignite the fine dust from the grain and cause an explosion. Next the malt is 'screened' in revolving drums which shake off the dust which is sucked away. The grain is then ground or milled into small pieces so that the sugar products can more easily be dissolved in water.

The mash tun at James Hole & Co.'s brewery.

The milled grain, or '*grist*' as it is now called, is then conveyed by hopper into the 'mash tun' where it is mixed with hot water to make a porridge-like mash. It remains in this state for two hours at a constant temperature of 65° - 67°C. The temperature is critical because that determines how well the enzymes in the malt convert the starch and proteins into sugars and amino acids. By the end of the mashing process, the sugars, amino acids and colouring matter will be dissolved in the hot water and formed into a sweet solution known as '*wort*'.

At the end of two hours, the wort is drained away through the floor of the mash tun, leaving the remaining grain to be '*sparged*' or sprinkled with more hot water (at 80°C) to remove as much sweet wort as possible. In a modern brewery, the *mashing* is done in a mash mixer and the extraction is done in an *lauter tun* - a longer but more efficient process.

The Fermenting Room at James Hole & Co.'s brewery.

Following removal from the mash tun, the wort is transferred to a *copper* or series of coppers. Here, the wort is boiled with hops for about two hours (the time depends on the type of beer being brewed). At this stage, sugar and *caramel* may be added. The boiling is important for, as well as extracting the flavour of the hops, any protein matter and enzymes, which might produce a haze or cloudiness in the final product, are destroyed, as are fungi and bacteria, and so the wort is sterilised.

The wort and hops are then passed to a '*hopback*' or, in a modern brewery, a 'whirlpool' where the hops are removed. The hopped wort is then pumped over a refrigeration system where it is cooled to 15°C and aerated with sterile air or oxygen ready for the addition of the yeast in the fermenting room.

The fermenting room was probably the most impressive area of a brewery. At Hole's Brewery in Newark, the fermenting room contained 20 fermenting vessels, 13 of which held 80 barrels each, and 3 held 170 barrels each. With 36 gallons per barrel, this was a total capacity of 55,800 gallons (253,600 litres) - nearly half a million pints. Approximately 1 kilogram of yeast is required to ferment 360 litres of wort, and fermentation is started by adding or 'pitching' the yeast. During fermentation, the yeast multiplies fourfold and converts the sugar in the wort to alcohol, producing large amounts of carbon dioxide, some of which can be collected, liquefied and later added to the beer to produce sparkle. The time taken for fermentation differs for ales and *lagers*. Ale yeasts take about 6 days at 12° - 18°C whilst lager yeasts ferment much more slowly (at 8° - 12°C) and take up to 3 weeks. The excess yeast builds up, on the surface, a deep froth which can be removed by suction. It is then dried and sold for food production and, because it is high in B vitamins, it is particularly useful in health foods (In modern breweries the fermentation process takes place in enclosed vats so the spectacular build up of froth can no longer be seen).

After fermentation, the beer must be matured or 'conditioned'. This takes place in *casks* which traditionally were wooden but now are aluminium or stainless steel. The process of barrelling is called *'racking'* and at this point, a double handful of best hops can be added through the bung hole (dry hopping). A small amount of yeast still remains in the beer and, with the addition of some sugar (primings), this now causes a secondary fermentation and gives the beer sparkle as it produces carbon dioxide.

Brewery conditioned beer is stored in large tanks holding several thousand litres and is kept for differing lengths of time depending on whether it is ale (1 week), lager or barley wine (4

The Racking Room at James Hole & Co.'s brewery with Mr Arthur Richmond (Brewery Foreman) on the right.

weeks). During this time, the sediment of solid material, like the remnants of the yeast and proteins, sinks to the bottom leaving the bright beer which is filtered off to await packaging in kegs, bottles and cans. Because it has been filtered, this type of beer keeps better and is more suitable for bottling and canning when it is required to have a long shelf life. Beer in glass bottles and cans is pasteurised to kill any micro-organisms which might spoil it. Beer for kegs and plastic bottles is flash heated before filling. So important is cleanliness in this process that the containers are flushed out with sterile carbon dioxide as they are filled, to prevent any last minute contamination with airborne bacteria.

Alcohol

Most beers contain about 4% alcohol, although some, for example barley wine, may contain up to 11%. Wines contain 10-15% alcohol with fortified wines (eg sherry) about 20%. Spirits contain about 40% alcohol. Low alcohol beers contain less than 1.2%, meaning that no excise duty is payable on them. The reduction of the alcohol content is achieved by removing the alcohol from normal beer or by reducing the amount produced during fermentation by cooling the wort to make the yeast inactive or reducing the amount of sugar available for fermentation.

Additives

Good brewers of the 19th Century prided themselves on producing beer from only the basic raw materials of malt, hops, yeast and water (and sugar) but today preservatives are added to kill microbes. Similarly, colour adjusters (eg *caramel*) may be added to give consistent colour, whilst antioxidant ascorbic acid is added to prevent 'off flavours' developing. Foam stabilisers, such as alginate esters, may also be added to ensure that the finished article possesses a rich, creamy head.

4. EARLY BREWING IN NEWARK

As discussed in Chapter 1, it was not until the 17th Century that large scale brewing companies made their appearance. Before that time people brewed their own ale or beer, as did the individual alehouses and inns. Usually the actual brewing process was the job of the women of the household and evidence of this is found in a record of the 'Tolsester Court of Brewers, Tipplers and Hucksters of the Town of Newark, held there on the Monday after the Feast of Mary Magdalene, 1567', when one Robert Simpson, 'because his wife is a common brewer and sells ale against the assize' was fined 12d (5p) and Nicholas Godderd, a tanner, was fined 4d 'because his wife is a common tippler' selling ale with unstamped vessels. Two other women were also fined 4d each for similar offences - Widow Swallow and Wife Plattes.

Those who are described in the Court Rolls as 'common brewers' frequently had other business interests, a trend which continued well into the 19th Century. John Houghton for example sold salt,candles and victuals 'against the assize' as well as being a common brewer.

Court records also reveal the cost of ale and showed that it was a serious offence to sell short measures. For example, in 1659 Robert White, a common brewer and seller of ale at Girton, was found guilty of not selling a full quart of ale for a penny 'according to the statute' and was fined 4 shillings (20p). In 1654 Goodwin Foreman and William Crosly, common brewers at Coddington, were fined 4d for not selling their 'ayle according to ye statute'.

By the end of the 17th Century, Newark had already gained a reputation for producing good beer as witnessed by the intrepid traveller, Celia Fiennes. In her diary of 1697 she says at Newark 'I met with the strongest and best Nottingham ale that looked very pale but exceedingly clear'.

In 1753 an Act was passed which stipulated that all those who wished to sell beer, cider, perry or spirits, whether sold for consumption on or off the premises, had to apply for a licence from the Justices. An applicant for a licence, if he had not been granted one the previous year, had to produce a certificate as to character, from the clergy,

Extract from a list of brewers and tipplers in Newark in the sixteenth century. For transcript, see Appendix III.

church wardens and overseers of the poor of the parish where he lived, or from three or four householders. Such licences could only be granted at the special Brewster Sessions held once a year. The Court records contain many instances of failure to comply with the laws relating to the keeping of ale houses, an example being that of William Cooling, a labourer, who on 4th October 1775 was fined 20 shillings (£1) for causing trouble by keeping a 'common ill governed and disorderly house at Girton and for causing and permitting men and women to remain there drinking, tippling, whoring and misbehaving themselves'. Since he refused to pay or find sureties, he was ordered to be committed to the House of Correction until the debt was discharged. Unfortunately there is no record of the outcome.

5. WHY DID NEWARK BECOME A 'BREWING TOWN'?

Three main factors contributed to the development of Newark as an important brewing centre. These were, firstly, a flourishing and long established malting industry with easy access to high quality barley supplies; secondly the town's location on the River Trent with easy access to the network of inland waterways, coastal ports and overseas trade; and thirdly, the availability of an exceptionally pure supply of water containing exactly the right amount of calcium sulphate (gypsum) - perfect for the brewing of excellent bright beers, comparable with those of Burton-on-Trent.

SAMUEL SKETCHLEY (*c*.1741-1831), was the 'Father' of Newark's brewing industry. He arrived from Burton-on-Trent in about 1766 and opened a brewery at the Town Wharf, in premises leased from the Duke of Newcastle. Although he was young (only about 25 when he arrived in Newark), he seems to have inspired considerable respect and confidence amongst his peers, and in 1769, after only 3 years in the town, was appointed a church warden. In the 1770s, Sketchley entered into a partnership with William Handley of Newark (a noted local banker) to establish a cotton mill off Mill Lane. The Mill was of considerable size with up to 300 employees supplying

Samuel Sketchley's house on Castlegate, was described as 'overlooking Trent Bridge'.

cotton thread to the Manchester linen trade. They were later joined in the business by Henry Jessop and a Mr Marshall. At the brewery, meanwhile, ledger entries for the years 1794-96 include many local customers, but it is clear that these Newark ales also travelled far and wide: shipments are noted to have departed for both Edinburgh and London.

With the poor quality of roads – including the Great North Road through Newark – such long distance deliveries would have been made by water. Barges would have first carried the beer down the River Trent to Hull where it was transferred to sea-going coastal vessels bound for the ports of London and Edinburgh.

It was not uncommon for the beer traffic to be balanced on the return journey up the Trent by cargoes of Baltic oak (imported to Hull), used for making beer cask staves. Thus, by 1784, in addition to Sketchley and Handley's brewing interests, they were also being listed as 'Raff Merchants', Raff being a term used to describe 'foreign timber'.

Samuel Sketchley was twice Mayor of Newark (in 1791 and 1804) and was also elected an Alderman in 1819. He lived with his wife, Elizabeth (née Ley, also from Burton-on-Trent) in a house on Castlegate, overlooking Trent Bridge, until 1808 when she died. Samuel died in December 1831 at the great age of 90. Both are commemorated by inscriptions in the south transept of the Parish Church.

6. EARLY NEWARK BREWERIES

The earliest Newark breweries were located along the River Trent which, as well as providing easy access for the great quantities of fuel required for the brewing process, also afforded easy long distance transport for the products, to inland and overseas markets.

Town Wharf Brewery

It would appear that Newark's first brewery (Handley and Sketchley's) was quick to attract attention in the brewing world, developing a thriving trade not only in this country but also abroad in northern Europe and Russia. Shilton, in his *History of Newark* (1820) states that during the reign of the Empress Catherine (1729-1796) the trade was extensive 'as she was extremely partial to stout humming ale'. When the Russian government levied heavy duty on imported British beer however, the trade was badly affected and the Town Wharf Brewery began to concentrate on its home market.

The surviving portion of Newark's first purpose-built brewery on the Town Wharf.

William Handley died in 1798, and in 1800 Samuel Sketchley retired from the business and the partnership (which had expanded to become William Handley, Samuel Sketchley, John Youle, John Reynoldson and James Wilson, merchants, ale and porter brewers) was dissolved. The business was continued by William Handley's youngest brother, Benjamin, John Youle and John Reynoldson. By 1802 William Farnsworth Handley and his brother John, had joined the business. The partnership with John Reynoldson was dissolved in 1808, leaving the Handley brothers in control. The business continued in the Handley family until 1856 when it was bought by

Handley House, Northgate, home of the owners of the Town Wharf Brewery.

Richard Warwick, who had become manager of the Handleys' Newark bank and later of the Wharf Brewery. He established a partnership with his eldest son, William Deeping Warwick as Richard Warwick and Son and continued trading at the Town Wharf Brewery until about 1872 when the first phase of their new brewery on Northgate was complete and ready for operation. About 1870, his second son, Richard Huskinson Warwick was appointed a partner and the firm then traded as Richard Warwick and Sons.

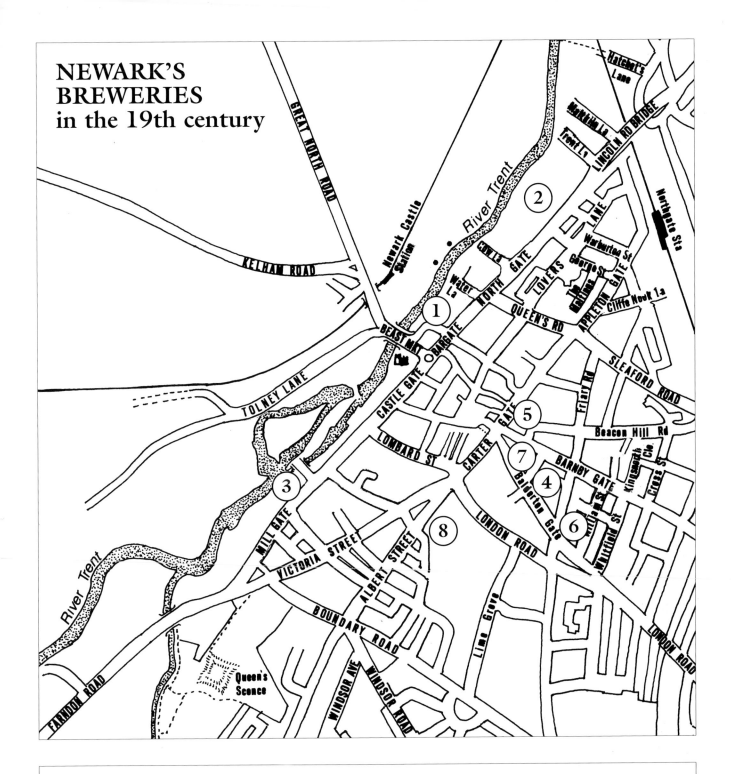

NEWARK'S BREWERIES
in the 19th century

KEY:
1. TOWN WHARF BREWERY
2. NORTHGATE BREWERY
   (WARWICKS & RICHARDSON'S)
3. TRENT BREWERY
4. OLIVER CROMWELL BREWERY
5. RUTLAND BREWERY
6. ALBION BREWERY
7. GOODWINS/DEVON BREWERY
8. CASTLE BREWERY
   (JAMES HOLE & CO.)

Advertisement for William Boler's Victoria Brewery from The Newark Times, 13th May 1840.

The Trent Brewery, Millgate

As early as 1802, Land Tax assessments refer to the site occupied by the Trent Brewery as Brewery Yard. In 1840 W. Boler operated his Victoria Brewery on the site (listed as Pond Yard Wharf - see advert). White's Directory for 1844 names Howe, Trusswell and Berry as holding the Trent Brewery in Millgate while Slater's Directory for 1850 names the owner as Abraham Howe and Company. By 1853, the brewery had passed into the hands of John Madin and Company, being purchased in 1857 by Messrs. Richardson, Earp and Slater.

A glimpse of these early days at the brewery may be obtained from an account given in the *Newark Advertiser* on 15th January 1862 concerning the 'usual annual supper' given by Richardson, Earp and Slater to their employees. It was held at the Swan and Salmon Inn on Castlegate, where 'the efforts of the worthy host and hostess in catering for the company gave the utmost satisfaction. The Chair was occupied by Mr Earp. The only cause of disappointment was the absence of Mr Richardson, who is at present away from home on account of ill health'. The account concludes with the comment that 'arrangements are now being made to enable the brewery to produce twice the quantity of ale which has hitherto been brewed there, the extension of the business having rendered such a course imperative'.

As will be seen from the plan on page 16, which was produced in 1888, the brewery covered a large site. It extended from Millgate, where the offices were situated, to the river frontage, where loads of coal could easily be delivered and barrels of beer despatched by barges to Nottingham, Hull and beyond. Beer was also sent by the new Midland and Great Northern Railways to Lincoln, Doncaster and other major centres.

The Millgate site included cooperage, bottling stores and stables, a boiler house, brewhouse, cooler room,

The Trent Brewery, photographed from its Millgate entrance in 1926. Brewing had ceased on the site in the late 1880s.

The Trent Brewery's trademark, based on the town's coat of arms, still in place at the entrance to the brewery in 1985 when this picture was taken.

loading shed, malthouse and extensive cellars as well as a watchman's cottage and office.

In 1884, the brewer in charge at the Trent Brewery was James, second son of Joseph Richardson. In that year he left and went to South America where, it is said, he mismanaged the sale of the Trent Brewery beers. His successor in Newark was T.W. Lovibond, who continued as brewer until 1887 when he went to Reid's Brewery in Newcastle.

In 1885 Thomas Earp retired from the Trent Brewery (where he had never been a particularly active partner) to concentrate his efforts in the malting firm of Gilstrap and Earp and as Liberal MP for the Borough of Newark. Thomas Earp was unusual in having Liberal views as most top brewers of this period were of the Tory persuasion.

At the same time, William Slater also left but continued as part owner of the Saracen's Head Hotel in Newark's Market Place. This left the Richardsons, Joseph and Charles, in charge of the Trent Brewery. The partnership was finally dissolved in 1888.

In 1888 the Duke of Newcastle, who owned the brewery premises, sold them together with many other properties that he owned within the town. In anticipation of the sale, the Richardsons were planning to build another brewery and bought land for this between the Northgate Brewery (Warwicks') and Bradley's Iron Foundry. On amalgamation with Warwick's however, the land was sold to them. In 1889 the Trent Brewery closed and the Richardsons entered partnership with Warwicks on Northgate. The cost of the Trent Brewery business to Warwicks was £55,042 5s 1d. The new business became Warwicks & Richardson's Ltd. and they adopted the Trent Brewery Company's trademark which was based on the Newark Borough coat of arms. The Millgate site was taken over by the firm of Wakes and Lamb (Wind Pump manufacturers) with the Trentside Buildings being finally demolished in 1952 when they had become unsafe owing to subsidence of the riverbank.

Trent Brewery, (c.1885).

Oliver Cromwell Brewery, Barnby Gate

The Oliver Cromwell Brewery was established in about 1869 by James Hooton. The *Newark Advertiser* of 5th July 1871 records 'another fire at the Cromwell Tavern' and describes how a fire in Mr Hooton's premises endangered the adjoining brewery with the loss of 150-200 barrels of various sizes and 13

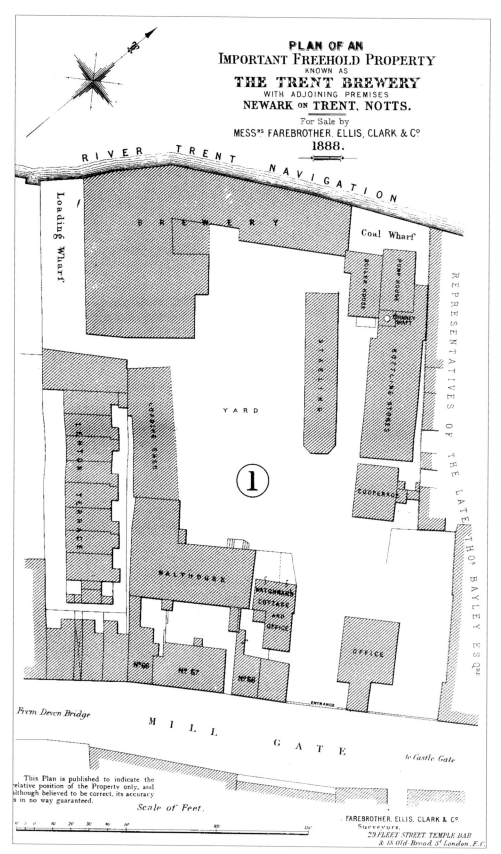

Architect's Plan of the Trent Brewery, 1888.

16

1.

JAMES HOLE & CO.

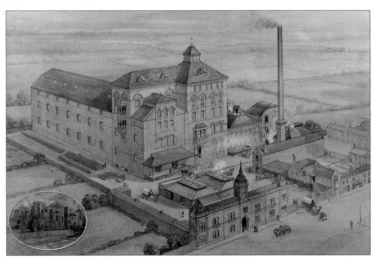

3.

2.

1. *Stone pediment depicting Newark Castle on the former office building.*

2. *Portrait of James Hole, Chairman of the Company from 1890-1914.*

3. *Nineteenth Century painting of Hole's Brewery.*

4. *Illustration on the front of a booklet about Hole's Brewery, showing one of their public house signs.*

4.

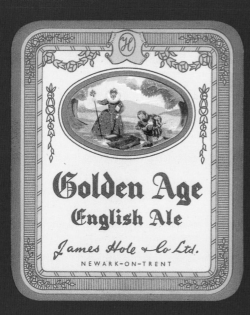

*Bottle Labels
from
James Hole & Co's
Castle Brewery*

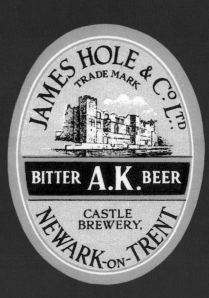

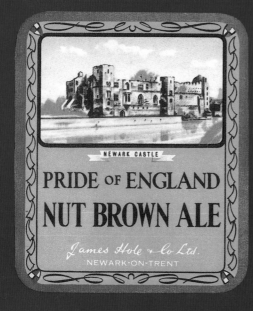

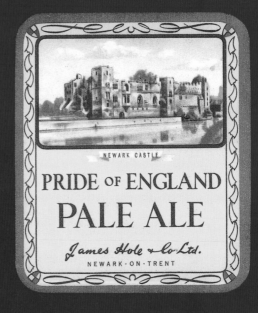

pockets of hops. The damage was estimated at between £350 and £400.

The brewery eventually came into the hands of the Smith family but in 1884, with the death of Mr. J.W. Smith, the partnership controlling the Cromwell Brewery was dissolved. The firm of Smith and Son ceased to have an interest in the brewery and all the property of the Cromwell Brewery Company was sold on 9th July 1884. The *Newark Advertiser* describes Lot 1 of the Sale as 'all that copyhold brewery known as the Oliver Cromwell Brewery with the brewery offices, blacksmith's and carpenter's shops, stables, sheds and other buildings, extensive yard and premises now in the occupation of Mr William Moss'.

William Moss appears to have acquired the brewery as a result of the sale, for on the 4th February 1885, the *Newark Advertiser* displayed an advertisement for the 'Cromwell Brewery's Pure Ales at 1s, 1s 2d, and 1s 4d per gallon, orders received by William Moss, 83 Barnby Gate, Newark and at the brewery'. The ales and stouts were available in casks up to 36 gallons (162 litres) or bottled in pints or half pints. The Company was also agent for the Greek Archipelago Pure Wine Company and Max Gregers celebrated Gaditano Sherries.

In 1889, Jessop and Hopewell of the Rutland Brewery (see below) purchased the business of L.C. Barstow and Co. Cromwell Brewery and formed the 'Newark Brewery Company'. This traded until 1891 when it was amalgamated with Messrs H.W. Robinson and Co. of Scotland Street, Sheffield as the Newark & Sheffield Breweries Ltd. This was acquired by Warwicks & Richardson's in 1892.

The Rutland Brewery, Barnby Gate

The Rutland Brewery was situated behind the Rutland Arms Hotel for which it brewed, as well as for private houses and free public houses. In 1884 part of the brewery premises were purchased by the trustees of Barnby Gate Wesleyan Chapel (which they also adjoined) for conversion to a new Sunday School classroom.

Morris' Directory for 1869 records John Wallis as proprietor of the Rutland Brewery as does White's in 1872. By 1881 it had been acquired by Robinson & Co. and by 1883, it was in the hands of H. Jessop. In 1889 the owners were Jessop and Hopewell, who in that year purchased the Cromwell Brewery from L.C. Barstow, forming the Newark Brewery Company.

Advertisement for William Moss' Cromwell Brewery, from The Newark Advertiser, 2nd January 1884.

NEWARK'S BREWERIES

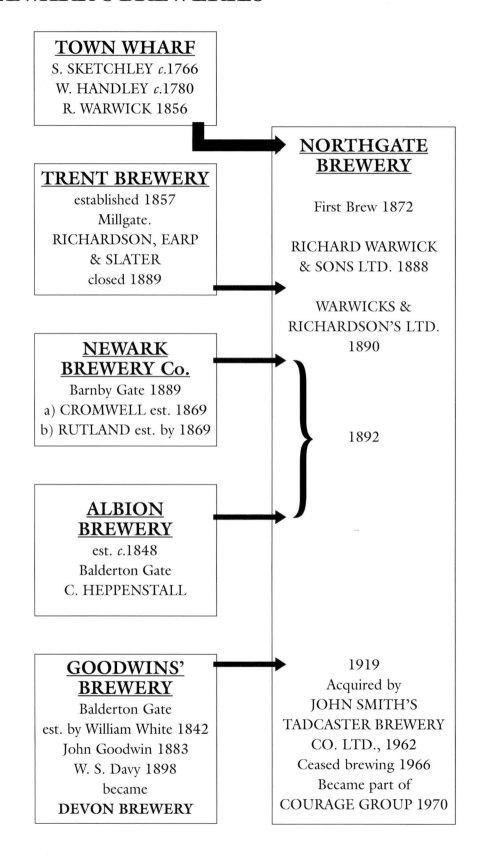

CASTLE BREWERY

Small brewery
in Albert Street
*c.*1870

CAPARN–HANKEY
New Offices *c.*1883

JAMES HOLE
bought 1885

New Brewery
1890

Taken over by
COURAGE, BARCLAY,
SIMONDS, 1968.
Merged with
JOHN SMITH'S
in 1970.
Ceased brewing 1982

TOWN WHARF
S. SKETCHLEY *c.*1766
W. HANDLEY *c.*1780
R. WARWICK 1856

TRENT BREWERY
established 1857
Millgate.
RICHARDSON, EARP
& SLATER
closed 1889

NEWARK BREWERY Co.
Barnby Gate 1889
a) CROMWELL est. 1869
b) RUTLAND est. by 1869

ALBION BREWERY
est. *c.*1848
Balderton Gate
C. HEPPENSTALL

GOODWINS' BREWERY
Balderton Gate
est. by William White 1842
John Goodwin 1883
W. S. Davy 1898
became
DEVON BREWERY

NORTHGATE BREWERY

First Brew 1872

RICHARD WARWICK
& SONS LTD. 1888

WARWICKS &
RICHARDSON'S LTD.
1890

1892

1919
Acquired by
JOHN SMITH'S
TADCASTER BREWERY
CO. LTD., 1962
Ceased brewing 1966
Became part of
COURAGE GROUP 1970

Albion Brewery, Balderton Gate

In the years 1848 to 1850, Christopher Heppenstall (b.1811) raised capital to buy land in an area bordered by Balderton Gate and an 'intended street', William Street. He built the Albion Brewery and the Eagle Tavern, starting his business in 1850. He purchased beerhouses: The Black Horse (later The Dolphin and then The Volunteer) in Barnby Gate (1851); the Victoria Inn, Balderton Gate (1860); the Marquis of Granby on Beacon Hill and the White Horse on Millgate (1872). He also acquired the Plough Inn at Egmanton and became the copyhold tenant of the Wheatsheaf at Farnsfield.

Christopher Heppenstall died in 1872 and his nephews, Christopher Heppenstall (b.1832) and the Rev. Frederick Heppenstall (b.1835) inherited the Albion Brewery business. In an unsettled period, the Rev. Frederick, a Headmaster in Cambridge, sold his half-holding in the brewery and the Eagle Tavern to Christopher for £1500. In 1876, however, he is still listed as owner of the Horse and Jockey in Newark and continued to share the ownership of other properties in the town with Christopher. The Rev. Frederick died in 1879, although trustees continued to manage his affairs thereafter.

From The Newark Advertiser, 20th July 1892.

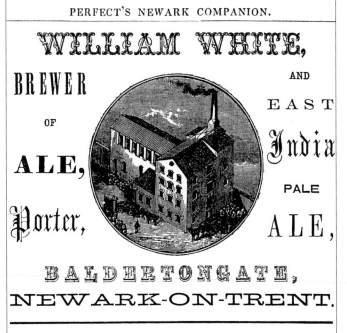

From Perfect's Newark Companion, 1865.

For his part in 1876, Christopher became lessee of the 'Boat' lodging house in Water Lane. In 1879 he also owned The Plough in Guildhall Street. His advertisements for the Albion Brewery at this time speak of 'ales and porter in splendid condition . . . from one shilling a gallon.' He also sold wines and spirits.

Christopher Heppenstall died in 1886, aged 54, owing £2788.0s.7d. His sons, Harold Wood Heppenstall and Christopher, were asked to 'convey' to the Bank the value of the Heppenstall properties, £4,600. The valuation indicated a balance in credit. The Company, 'Heppenstall Brothers', survived but in 1890 they elected to become a Limited Company. Profits increased although plans to increase beer production came to nothing.

In 1892 Warwicks & Richardson's made an agreement with the Company. Heppenstalls concentrated on the wine and spirit trade, joining with McGeorge & Sons in that year to become 'McGeorge & Heppenstalls', when 'Newark Beer' was supplied by Warwicks & Richardson's to the company. By 1895, the Albion Brewery had ceased brewing.

McGeorge & Heppenstalls survived anxious times until 1924 when successive increases in Duty had caused 'insurmountable difficulties'. The Brewers Warwicks & Richardson's, were granted a lease of the Company's freehold properties at a meeting of McGeorge and Heppenstalls on 6th March 1924.

Goodwins' Brewery, Balderton Gate

The Brewery in Balderton Gate which became known as 'Goodwins', was originally in the hands of William White, who established it in 1842. He is described in Morris and Co.'s Directory for 1869 as 'brewer and maltster' of Balderton Gate and Royal Oak Inn, Castlegate, (an 1853 Directory describes him as holding the Royal Oak Brewery, Castlegate). White brewed both for public houses, and for private trade. He also bottled a considerable amount of Guinness stout. After White's death, his widow, Dinah, took her bottling trade back to the Royal Oak in Castlegate. In 1884 she transferred the lease of

Messrs. Goodwin Bros. brewery, Balderton Gate, showing the extensions which had been built after 1883. Compare this illustration with that on page 19, when the brewery was owned by William White. From The Newark Advertiser, 28th January 1891.

the Balderton Gate Brewery to John Goodwin, who had formerly worked at the Castle Brewery in Albert Street (see page 29). In the Duke of Newcastle's great sale of 1888, Mrs White bought the Ram Hotel and left the Royal Oak. She continued her Guinness trade at The Ram until her death in 1898.

The Devon Brewery's nameplate may still be seen in Barnby Gate, where the company had its front offices (opposite the Methodist Church).

John Goodwin was a Managing partner of Caparn and Hankey's Castle Brewery on Albert Street, moving to take over the Whites' Brewery just before the Castle Brewery was acquired by James Hole and Co. When he took over the Balderton Gate Brewery in 1883, its output was less than 4,000 barrels per year, but he so extended its premises and its trade that eight years later, the output had risen to 12,273 barrels. In 1891 Messrs. Goodwin Brothers became a limited company, owning in addition to the brewery (which now extended from Balderton Gate through to Barnby Gate), 28 freehold, copyhold and leasehold public houses and 7 freehold dwelling houses. The whole of the property was valued at £40,500. New offices at the Barnby Gate entrance to the property were acquired in 1891, as was a new and extensive boiler-room with a new boiler by Hawkesley Wild & Co. of Sheffield.

The brewery drew its water from what was described as 'an underground reservoir, yielding an inexhaustible flood of the finest brewing water to be found anywhere'. Three sets of powerful pumps were erected to distribute this supply throughout the premises. By the early 1890s the brewery was further extended with the introduction of a new plant for the production of a 'semi-lager' beer called Amber Ale.

John Goodwin died on 24th November 1896 and, for a while, the brewery was carried on by his sons, William and Fleming. However by 9th March 1898, Mr Walter Shirley Davy had taken it over and re-named it the 'Devon Brewery' (pronounced 'De*e*von', in common with the local river). Like John Goodwin before him, W. S. Davy had first served as a manager at the Castle Brewery on Albert Street before taking over sole proprietorship of the Balderton Gate premises. Having acquired Goodwins' Brewery, Davy continued to expand the business until 1919 when it was merged

Cross Keys Inn, Beaumond Street (c.1914). The inn is known today as The Mail Coach.

with Warwicks & Richardson's Ltd. Mr Davy joined the Board of the latter company but was asked to resign two years later. (The circumstances of his resignation are not recorded, but he subsequently became Chairman of Messrs Truswells' Brewery at Sheffield). Some of the Devon Brewery buildings were used for stabling Warwicks & Richardson's dray horses, although the brewing equipment remained in place until as late as the 1950s. Some of the buildings were eventually sub-let to Lacey & Sons, painters and decorators, Duckerings Hardware (later Jackson & Shipley) and Partners Press.

Above: The George & Dragon, Castlegate (c.1890).

Left: The Victoria Inn, Balderton Gate (c.1920).

7. WARWICKS & RICHARDSON'S, NORTHGATE

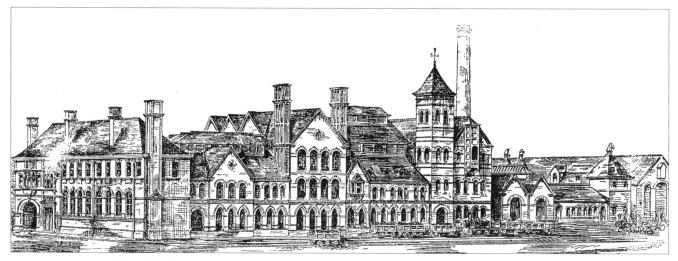

Warwicks & Richardson's brewery, offices and maltings, Northgate, as they appeared in 1890.

This was Newark's longest lived brewery, having its origins in Handley and Sketchley's Town Wharf Brewery in c.1766. Warwicks & Richardson's eventually absorbed all the breweries mentioned above.

In 1856 Richard Warwick, whose father, William, had been manager of the Handleys' Newark bank, purchased the Handleys' brewing interest in the town. The Town Wharf Brewery at this time had become somewhat run-down, producing only 4,360 barrels annually as opposed to the 7,500 it had been achieving 60 years previously. To Richard Warwick, however, the brewery's potential was clear. Working in partnership with his eldest son, William Deeping Warwick, Richard continued to trade at the Town Wharf Brewery until *c.*1872.

In 1863, Richard Warwick bought about 1½ acres of land in Northgate and in 1864 a small, elegantly styled malting was erected on part of the Northgate site. The site was eventually increased to about 11 acres and, in 1871, the first phase of the new Northgate Brewery was begun, including a spur line to the Midland Railway and the Great Northern Railway. The first brew at the new brewery took place on 14th September 1872.

Richard Warwick's new brewery on Northgate under construction, early 1870s.

Richard Warwick died in 1877 leaving William Deeping Warwick as senior partner in the firm. On 1st July 1888, the business was incorporated as Richard Warwick & Sons Ltd., a title which included Richard's second son, Richard Huskinson Warwick who had become a partner about 1870.

The Trent Brewery Company was acquired in 1890 and incorporated as Warwicks & Richardson's Ltd. This was followed by the acquisition of The Newark Brewery in 1892, Stone's Home Brewery of Peterborough (1897), Alfred Eadon & Co. Ltd., Doncaster (1897), Morris' Rutland Brewery Co., Oakham, Rutland (1906), Alma Brewery, Cambridge (1911), W.S. Davy, Devon Brewery, Newark (1919), McGeorge and Heppenstalls (1924), Brampton Brewery Co. Ltd., Brampton, Chesterfield

(1955) and Smith & Co. (Oundle) Ltd., North Street Brewery, Oundle, Northants (1955). In 1962 however, Warwicks & Richardson's Ltd., was itself acquired by John Smith's Tadcaster Brewery Co. Ltd. and ceased brewing in 1966. The latter company became part of the Courage Group in 1970 and is now incorporated within Scottish and Newcastle plc.

The front offices of Warwicks & Richardson's brewery, designed by the architect William Bliss Sanders.

The Brewery

The *Newark Advertiser* of 9th April 1890, devoted considerable space to its coverage of the building of the new offices of Warwicks & Richardson's, including two architect's drawings (by William Bliss Sanders of South Kensington). The 'capacious' offices to house clerks and directors of the company, were to be of red brick, roofed with Broseley tiles and built by Mr Baines of Newark. They were the final phase of the 'splendid' brewery which, by 1890, employed 133 people, including 93 in the brewery and 40 clerks and travellers. The brewing capacity was nearly 100,000 barrels a year with strong, pale & mild ales and stouts being produced.

Most of the malt required was produced by the firms own maltings, some of which, built in 1864 in the 'semi-Grecian style', adjoined the brewery. After passing through screening and cleaning machines, the malt was crushed by steel rollers and passed into two cast iron mash tuns, six feet high, one of 43 quarters (547 kilograms) and the other 22 quarters (280 kilograms) capacity. With the addition of spring water from Beacon Hill springs 1½ miles away, where the company had a pumping station, the liquor ran via pipes into two wort coppers heated by steam jackets and containing adjustable fountains and a third one heated by fire. Here the hops were added. Each copper held 120 barrels. After boiling, the liquor was conveyed in pipes to hop-backs which retained the hops and allowed the beer to be pumped to the cooling rooms. The vast quantity of water required for cooling and washing was obtained from a well 90ft deep (27 metres) within the premises, and was pumped at the rate of 15,000 gallons (approximately 68,100 litres), per hour up to a great cistern.

After cooling, the liquor was fermented in one of three rooms, the most recent of which was 87ft (26 metres) in length and 60ft (18 metres approximately) wide, with three box-louvered roofs. Finally the beer was racked and stored in cellars capable of holding 4,000 barrels of ale.

Transport

Horse drawn drays belonging to the local breweries must have been a very common sight in Newark in the second half of the nineteenth century and the early part of the twentieth. There is an interesting little book in the Tadcaster Archives entitled 'Foreman Jordan's Journeys', containing reports on the horses of Warwicks & Richardson's Brewery and their welfare in 1914.

It seems that Foreman Jordan was in overall charge of all the horses used by the Warwick Group of Breweries and his duties included visiting all the depots every four to six weeks and reporting not only on the health of the horses but the maintenance of their tack and the carts. On 19th September 1914, the Nottingham Team 'Carlos', 'Dulverton' and 'Peary', he commented, 'were looking thin through overwork. Would like a little more food for them'. By 4th December, he reported that they were satisfactory. At Mansfield, the horse 'Star' was 'going stiff on off hind leg through overwork, do not think it is serious. Told drayman to take care of him and if any worse to report'. At Goole, on 8th January 1916, he commented on the horses, 'Bill', 'Sappho' and 'Wellington', 'they are running

The barrel yard at Warwicks & Richardson's.

these horses off their legs, they put one of them in the gig one day and into the lorry next day to deliver the goods, which is too much. They will have to have another cob unless they get the railway company to cart goods to the stores'.

The horses were frequently moved about (by rail) from town to town to wherever they were needed. Shorter journeys, for example Lincoln to Newark, were undertaken by road.

The names of some of the Warwick horses were:

Ardwisp, Mafeking, Leopard, Marlborough, Croydon, Lady Quarrington, Rauceby, Kate, Polly (who produced a foal - May), Staythorpe, Charlie, Messina, Jersey, Julia, Nightingale, Sunbeam, Daisy, Alpha, Nancy, Emperor, Dublin, Jericho, Bilsthorpe, Egypt, Paris, Jessy and Haig.

Delivery lorries at Warwicks & Richardson's Brewery.

The horses were stabled at the old Town Wharf brewery buildings and the stable foremen in 1890 were: J. Pearson, Cragg, Mellows, Brooks, Lawson, Bagguley, Holland, Hickman, T. Pearson and Jordan. If any of these were away ill, or on holiday, men were called out of the cellar department to help. These included Andrews and Hartley. A note to John Pearson on 12th March 1890 instructs him, 'as soon as you can with safety turn horses out to grass, do so, and in that way reduce the number of horses kept at the Newark stables to the following:

17	Dray horses
2	Float
1	Traveller's horse
Totals 20	

The account books show that the majority of horses were dispensed with between 1920 and 1921.

Horse drawn delivery cart from Warwicks & Richardson's Brewery.

As mentioned above, following their acquisition of the Devon Brewery, Warwicks & Richardson's used some of the buildings for stabling their dray horses. These included six magnificent shire horses. Two were required to pull each of the two large drays and two smaller drays were pulled by single horses. In 1930 there were four draymen employed, including Joe Trowell, Sam Faulkner, Sam Kitchen and Harry Baumber, the foreman. They covered an area extending from Newark to Southwell and Collingham (greater distances were covered by 'Sentinal' steam wagons). Mr Vic Baumber, Harry's son, has vivid memories of being delivered to Mount School on the dray each morning as his father drove it to be loaded at the brewery in Northgate. He also remembers accompanying his father to take one of the 'gentle giants' to be shod by Mr Billy Southern, the blacksmith, at his smithy in William Street, and riding back down Barnby Gate 'on a charger fit to carry any knight into battle'.

Mr Baumber says the highlight of every week was Monday at 8.00 am when Colonel Philip Warwick and his son, Derick, came to inspect the horses. 'Even at my tender age' he says, 'I realised how much these gentlemen loved and admired these magnificent beasts.'

The coming of the Second World War and the march of transport modernisation brought the end of the horse-drawn drays and Harry Baumber became a brewery lorry driver.

The Fire Brigade

Fire was an ever present possibility in a brewery heating large quantities of liquor and requiring vast quantities of hot water and steam for cleansing. Many of the country's largest breweries invested in private engines, not wishing to rely on the often inadequate provision available in their towns. Interestingly, the Rules for Richard Warwick & Sons' Fire Brigade have survived in the archives of John Smith's Tadcaster Brewery (reproduced on page 26) showing that all the members had to live in Spital Row and were paid 5s. (25p) every three months. For each practice they received 1s 6d (7.5p) for the first hour and 6d (2.5p) per hour afterwards. For actual calls, Daymen received 1s. per hour if called out at nights and Nightmen received the same if called out during the day. Members who failed to arrive at the brewery Engine Room within a reasonable time (not specified) after the sounding of the Fire Alarm, were fined unless they could give a satisfactory reason. At the end of the year, the fines were equally divided amongst those members who had not been fined.

The main job of the Warwicks' Fire Brigade was to protect the brewery and this had been the reason for the purchase of the 'modern' Merryweather steam fire engine which they named 'Gertrude'. She was always kept in readiness complete with suction pipe permanently in position to draw from the river when 'at home' on the brewery premises. She could raise one hundred pounds of steam in five to six minutes and, to the great pride of the employees, was capable of throwing water over the brewery chimney shaft, 110ft (nearly 34 metres) high. With 440ft (135 metres) of leather hose and 750ft (230 metres) of canvas piping, it was ensured that she could reach even the most remote parts of the premises.

Alongside Gertrude in the engine room was a fire alarm in a glass case which, in the event of fire, was activated by the watchman. This in turn would set off electric bells in the firemen's bedrooms on Spital

RD. WARWICK & SONS'

FIRE BRIGADE.

✦ RULES. ✦

1.—Members must attend any Fire that may break out on the property of Rd. Warwick and Sons, and at the houses of any of the Partners; and all Practices, unless told not to attend by the Superintendent or Deputy-Superintendent.

2.—No Member may leave a Fire or a Practice without permission from the Superintendent or Deputy-Superintendent

3.—No unnecessary talking will be allowed.

4.—Members not arriving at the Brewery Engine Room, which is the appointed place for all to meet, within reasonable time after the sounding of the Fire Alarm, will be fined, unless they can give a satisfactory reason.

5.—Members leaving the Brigade give or receive one week's notice on Tuesday night.

6.—Members leaving the Brigade, who occupy houses in Spital Row, will have to give them up within three weeks after leaving the Brigade.

7.—Members leaving their houses in Spital Row must also leave the Brigade.

8.—All Helmets, Coats, Belts, &c., are the property of Rd. Warwick & Sons.

9.—Members will be paid Five Shillings every three months.

10.—Fines will be inflicted in cases of misbehaviour or negligence, but no Member will be fined more than Five Shillings during three months.

11.—At the end of each year the fines will be equally divided amongst Members who have not been fined.

12.—For Practice during the Firm's time, no pay beyond their ordinary wages will be allowed.

13.—For Practice in the Member's time they will be paid Eight-pence for the first hour or part thereof, and at the rate of Six-pence per hour afterwards.

14.—If a Dayman is called out between 9 p.m. and 5 a.m., or a Nightman between 6 a.m. and 3 p.m., he will be paid One Shilling for the first hour or part thereof, and at the rate of Eight-pence per hour afterwards.

15.—Any Member intending to leave home for one or more nights, must inform the Superintendent or Deputy-Superintendent

16.—Members leaving Rd. Warwick & Sons' employ must leave the Fire Brigade.

17.—Members leaving the Fire Brigade need not on that account leave the Firm's employ.

Row. A steam operated horn was also sounded over the brewery premises. An alarm was also linked to the stables half a mile away at the old Town Wharf Brewery to summon the horses to be harnessed to the fire engine.

That the Warwicks' Fire Brigade was a valuable asset, not only to the brewery but also in attending fires around the town is shown by the numerous accounts of their activities in the *Newark Advertiser* in the 1880s and the letters of thanks received by the company from a number of grateful victims of fires. It seems that the Warwicks' Fire Brigade was better equipped than the town brigade, having a steam-driven fire engine, while the latter only had a hand operated one.

The *Newark Advertiser* for 12th September 1883 records a large fire on the property of Mr. William Duke, a Newark builder and contractor, who lived on a farm at Little Carlton. The bearings of a drum of a threshing machine had overheated and this resulted, during the night, in a very large fire destroying 14 stacks and various agricultural implements at an estimated value of £1,500-£2,000. It took an hour to gain the services of the Newark Fire Brigade, who did their best but with limited success. The fire continued to burn the next day when Warwicks' Fire Brigade were sent for. It's steam fire engine was capable of discharging 450 gallons of water a minute by 3 hoses and soon had the situation under control. The newspaper records that the Brigade was fully equipped with firemen's helmets, coats, leggings etc. and was under the direction of their Captain, Mr J. F. Warwick.

Warwicks did not like sending out their Fire Brigade into the town because it left their own premises at risk and jeopardised their position with the Insurance Companies. However, they continued to do so when called upon and it was not until the

A fireman from Warwicks & Richardson's brewery.

Autumn of 1886 that the Town Corporation gave serious consideration to the advantages of obtaining a steam fire engine of their own. This was the result of a disastrous night-time fire at Thomas Parnham's mill in Barnby Gate in August 1886. Almost the whole of the steam corn mill was destroyed and the neighbouring houses and the newly installed gas cylinders at the nearby gas works, were greatly endangered by both fire and falling debris. The reflection of the fire was so bright that it was said that those passing through the Market Place could plainly see the figures on the Parish Church clock. Again, the equipment of the Town Brigade under Superintendent Mr Charles Johnson, proved insufficient and the services of Warwicks' Fire Brigade had to be called upon. At first, low water pressure in that part of the town frustrated the Warwicks' brigade's efforts to master the blaze. A horseman was sent out to the water company at Muskham to request an increase in pressure and, with this done, the combined forces of the Town and Warwicks' fire engines eventually brought the blaze under control.

Such was the gratitude of the neighbouring householders that, following a meeting at the Vine Hotel, 230 signed an address of thanks to Mr J. F. Warwick (see page 28).

To John Francis Warwick Esq.

We the undersigned Owners and Occupiers of

Property in the vicinity of the late disastrous fire at Mr Parnham's Mill in Barnby Gate desire to tender you our sincerest thanks for the very timely and efficient aid rendered by you in preventing a further spread of outbreak &c which might have been fraught with more serious results to life and property.____

The generosity with which you lent your services to those of the Engine and Brigade to assist Mr Supt Johnson and the Newark Brigade merit our admiration and we beg to cordially thank you for the manner in which you promptly responded to an appeal for help which undoubtedly had the effect of saving valuable Property from further destruction.

Signed

H Parnham
M. Parnham
J. J. Parnham
L. M. Parnham
L. A Parnham
E. J. Parnham
pro Newark Gas Co
J. Daniel

Wil Parnham
R. W. Parnham
W. Grantham
J. J. Parnham
John Sims Nine Hotel
Thos Smith Saw Mill
John Hage
John J. Capam

8. CAPARN AND HANKEY, ALBERT STREET

This was the forerunner of Newark's other large brewery - The Castle - later James Hole's.

John Smith Caparn was descended from a family of shoemakers who, by the 19th Century, had risen in Newark's business and professional life. In 1869, J. S. Caparn established a malting company in Lombard Street, and by 1872 (according to White's Directory) he also owned the Robin Hood Brewery on the same site. He went into partnership with Joseph Bishell until 1878 and, in March 1879, in partnership with Mr Douglas Hankey, he bought the old workhouse and hospital site in Albert Street for £800.

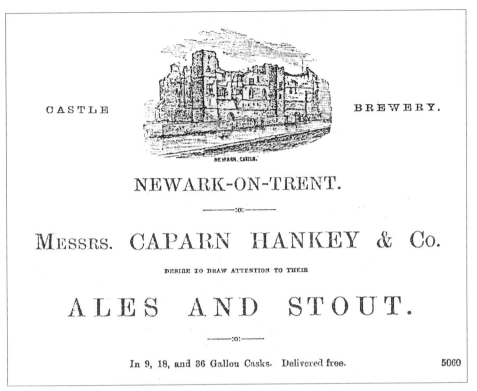

CASTLE BREWERY.

NEWARK-ON-TRENT.

———:o:———

MESSRS. CAPARN HANKEY & Co.

DESIRE TO DRAW ATTENTION TO THEIR

ALES AND STOUT.

———:o:———

In 9, 18, and 36 Gallon Casks. Delivered free.   5060

From The Newark Advertiser, 29th April 1885.

In June 1881, the foundation stone for the very grand offices fronting the site was laid by Miss Goodwin, sister of the Head Brewer, John Goodwin (later to become owner of the Balderton Gate Brewery). The Company traded under the name of 'Caparn, Hankey and Co.', although the actual partners were J.S. Caparn, Douglas Hankey, Herbert Maynard Hatfield and John Goodwin. By 1883, John Goodwin had left (to start his own brewery - see page 20) and J.S. Caparn had become a 'sleeping partner'. Fisher Hargreaves Coles Proctor's, Sales catalogue of 1992 described the offices thus – 'built in the French-Renaissance style, the imposing brewery offices exhibit a central clocktower, surmounted by a slate tower and cupola. It is supported on red composition doric pilasters beneath a dentil cornice. A pediment with a mural scene of Newark Castle adds a further touch of grace. At either end of the offices there are roof turrets with finials'.

The cost of the new offices was about £10,000 and in providing a building of such grandeur, Caparn and Hankey had over-reached themselves. The small brewery could not sustain such an outlay, with the result that the company went bankrupt. The premises were acquired by James Hole and Samuel Kercheval Marsland in 1885.

Brewery Offices built for Caparn and Hankey

9. JAMES HOLE & CO. LTD.: CASTLE BREWERY, ALBERT STREET

James Hole and Samuel Kercheval Marsland had already become established as leading maltsters in the town and both had been mayor when they formed a partnership to take over the Castle Brewery from the bankrupt Caparn, Hankey Co. in 1885.

The Castle Brewery on Albert Street. The distinctive offices were built for Caparn and Hankey in 1881 and taken over by James Hole & Co. four years later. This photograph dates from 1982, the year when beer production ceased at the brewery.

The site they acquired already had an interesting history. Part had been occupied by the old workhouse hospital and gaol (built 1785), whilst the remainder had been occupied by a starch factory, established there to take advantage of the same excellent source of water later to be exploited by the brewery. By 1890 the demand for Hole's beer had increased to such an extent that it was necessary to build a much larger brewery, one which was in keeping with the palatial offices. The new brewery was planned so carefully that it was possible to maintain production while the extensive building operations were carried out. First the new boiler house was built followed by a new brewhouse of local red bricks with moulded cornices, and internally faced with white glazed bricks to facilitate cleanliness.

The new brewhouse contained a horizontal steam engine on the ground floor, a spacious entrance lobby and a mill room where the malt was crushed. An elevator conveyed the grist to the grist case on the third floor.

On the first floor was the laboratory with a second floor containing cast iron mash tuns and associated equipment. On the third floor was a cast iron hot liquor tank, with iron grist case and vertical refrigerators, whilst the top floor was given over entirely to a large copper cooler.

To the left of the brewhouse stood the fermenting house with cellars extending under this and also under the brewhouse and copper house to the right. The fermenting tuns were on the first floor of the fermenting house with the second and third floors being used for malt storage.

The brewery yard at James Hole's Castle Brewery, photographed c.1889. Part of the old workhouse may be seen on the right.

The 'new brewery' at James Hole's Castle Brewery, commenced in 1890.

History

In 1890, the firm had become a private limited company and was joined by a third partner - in addition to James Hole and S.K. Marsland - Mr. Arthur Gilstrap Soames. The first Chairman was James Hole and the three Directors held all the shares. James Hole and S.K. Marsland were still carrying on their malting business and this continued until September 1934 when it was leased to Hugh Baird and Sons.

Mr. S.K. Marsland died in 1900 and Edward Kercheval Marsland, his son, joined the business. Mr. J. Reynolds Hole, son of Mr. James Hole, was also a Director. After James Hole's death in 1914, his place as Chairman was taken by Mr Arthur Gilstrap Soames.

In 1927 the firm bought the small Market Rasen Brewery with 33 of its licensed houses and in 1935, Messrs. Lowe, Son and Cobbold of Stamford, brewers and wine & spirit merchants were likewise taken over. In both cases, the breweries were dismantled.

In 1968 James Hole and Co. was taken over by Courage, Barclay, Simonds and in 1970 they merged with the John Smith's Group of companies which already included Warwicks & Richardson's. Mineral water production ended in the 1970s and the last brew at the Castle Brewery was in 1982. From 1971 to 1991 all the licensed houses which had previously belonged to Hole's and Warwicks & Richardson's were administered by John Smith's. After that date, Inntrepreneur became responsible for all the licensed houses in the Courage Group. The Castle Brewery offices closed in May 1991. The site was sold to a property development company but at the time of writing (1997), its future remains uncertain.

Scientific Brewing

In any brewery, the responsibility of obtaining excellence in the product is with the Head Brewer. By regarding the brewing process as an exact science, optimum results are produced at every stage and a consistently high standard is thus achieved. This was not always the case in the early days of brewing when brewers relied simply on experience or chance.

The Head Brewer's house (Beaumond Cross House) on London Road.

The Laboratory (left) and the home of Arthur Richmond (Head Foreman) overlooking Albert Street.

During the first half of the twentieth century, the brewery benefited from the expertise of a dynasty of 'scientific brewers' - the Heron family.

Mr Thomas Henry Heron, the Head Brewer for a considerable period during the first half of this century, was a nephew of a famous family of brewers who left Ireland to develop scientific brewing in England. Two sons of the family, John and Harold (cousins of Thomas Henry), became consultant brewers to the Castle Brewery and Thomas Henry's son, John Golding Heron, became third brewer before moving to Hertfordshire.

Hygiene

Cleanliness is a constant watch-word within the brewing trade and James Hole & Co. were particularly proud of the measures they took to ensure the perfection of their products.

Delivery vehicles in the yard at Hole's Castle Brewery in the mid 1920s.

One of their treasures was the Hills 'Correct Process' bottle cleaning machine invented by Mr. Thomas Hill of Baston, near Bourne, Lincolnshire and supplied by the Thomas Hill Engineering Co. (Hull) Ltd. When purchased, this was the most hygienic system available.

It was in the *cooper's* shop and barrel yard however, that the most scrupulous care was taken over cleanliness. Barrels were first washed out with hot water and then super-heated steam was blown through the water in the barrels to make it boil. They were then left in the water for some time before being placed on a rinsing machine which agitated them violently under a shower. After brushing, the barrels were emptied and finally sterilised by being inverted over jets of dry steam. After all this they were inspected by hand by the barrel yard foreman with an electric lamp and finally subjected to his nose to ensure there was no sour odour.

Elsewhere in the brewery, the high standard of cleanliness was maintained by pumice, cold water and elbow grease - no metal polish was allowed in the burnishing of coppers, mash tuns, vats or boilers for fear of contamination. Even hot water was banned in some areas as it might have encouraged oxidisation of the metal.

Transport

The emphasis on cleanliness, evident throughout the brewing process, was to be found even in the transport department. The fleet of 20 yellow Leyland lorries, which often travelled 200 miles per day, were always immaculate for their morning inspection, even under the bonnet. Each driver was responsible for his own lorry. Attention to detail in maintenance was rewarded by the presentation of a cup. Cash bonuses were also awarded to the men whose lorries were found to be in the best condition at the periodic inspections carried out by the Managing Director.

Engineering Shops

The Engineering Shops were responsible not only for the repair and maintenance of the lorries but also for all the mechanical and electrical equipment in the brewery. Under Mr. A.E. Knight, A.M.Inst.B.E. the brewery prided itself on being self-sufficient up to the coming of the Second World War.

The Staff

Hole's employees tended to remain with the firm for long periods of time - up to 50 years was not uncommon. It was said that every employee in the firm, whether in the offices or in the brewery itself, was personally known to Mr. Marsland, the Managing Director and could take any grievance straight to him. The well-being of employees and their dependants was of considerable importance to the firm. Not only was there a non-contributory pension scheme but also provision for recreation: a sports ground with tennis courts and bowling green adjacent to the brewery and, later, a cricket and football field on Muskham Road. In the 1950s the Castle Brewery football team played in the Spartan League. There was also a fishing association and a rifle club with annual outings for all the staff to such places as Skegness, Blackpool, London and even Amsterdam.

Directors and staff at James Hole & Co. Ltd., 16th June 1953:
From back row (L-R): S. Darcey, W. A. Marshall, A. Fisher, W. Weselby, J. T. Riley, D. Jackson.
A. W. Gosling, J. F. Pepper, G. E. Inskeep, J. H. Burley, H. Clarke, S. B. Weselby, A. E. Armstrong, W. Holmes.
H. Rushton, W. Trickett, J. Parr, F. Footitt, A. Richmond, H. Hooton, R. Pick, G. W. Cobb, W. J. Nash.
G. S. Cowley, R. Morewood, D. Murray, J. A. Tadman, J. E. Skinner, G. F. Wilson, G. Lidgett, R. J. Circuit, A. E. Rogers,
T. W. Dodgson.
W. M. Elverston-Trickett, Esq., S. Fairclough, Sir Oliver C. E. Welby, Bart., H. Shackleton, Captain A. Granville Soames, OBE,
R. E. Jones, G. C. Wadham, Esq., Miss M. E. Brown, Major H. W. Cairns M.C.

10. THE PRODUCT

The Newark water, like that of Burton-on-Trent, was primarily suited to the production of 'light ales' and it was these that earned both the town's great breweries widespread acclaim. Richard Warwick & Sons won a first class medal in the 1866 Dijon Exhibition and it was the Castle Brewery's 'AK' Luncheon Ale which gained them a Gold Medal at the International Brewing Exhibition in Paris in 1889.

In addition to light and mild ales, Holes also brewed 'BB Strong Ale' which was stored for 12 months, mainly in their cellars in St Mark's Lane, before being dispatched. These cellars also housed their India Pale Ales, a 'full-bodied nourishing beverage, pure and wholesome'. Both were brewed from malt and hops only.

Both of Newark's main breweries won many awards for their products.

11. BREWING IN NINETEENTH CENTURY CENSUS RECORDS

Table showing the development of Newark's Brewing Industry, 1851-1891

Census Year	Total Population	Brewers	Maltsters	Allied Trades (publicans, coopers, draymen etc.)	Other Occupations	Total in work
1851	11,330	18	98	71	4806	4993
1861	11,515	39	181	103	4785	5108
1871	12,195	64	206	128	4790	5188
1881	14,018	115	221	119	5443	5898
1891	14,457	168	267	124	5490	6049

Whilst these figures clearly chart the growth of the brewing and malting trades, it is unlikely that the totals shown reflect the true numbers working in those industries. There must have been many more labourers who actually worked in maltings or breweries but who did not (on the basis of seasonal or other variations) specify what kind of work they did. As far as the census goes they belonged to the vast army listed solely as 'general labourer'.

The above figures may be compared with the **county** statistics available for the twentieth century:

In 1911 there were 688 brewers and 659 maltsters in the **county**.
In 1966 there were 1,960 males and 450 females in malting and brewing in the **county**.

Development of Newark's Brewing Industry, 1851-1891

(Figures used from table above)

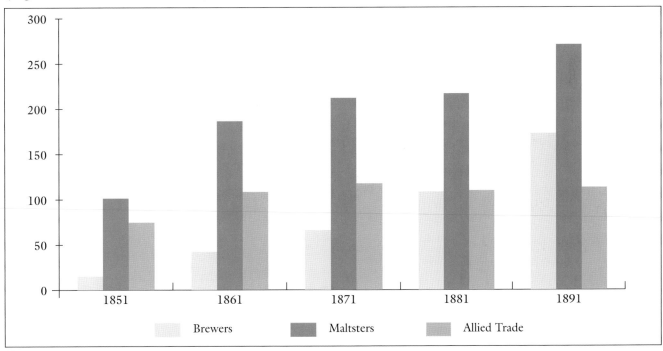

Newark Brewers listed in the 1861 Census

Name	Age	Type of Work
Adcock John	47	Brewer's clerk & Methodist preacher
Alcock George	17	Brewer
Brown William	62	Brewer
Brooks George	40	Brewer's labourer
Brewster James	24	Brewery storesman
Cooper Charles	55	Retired Brewer
Cree Joseph	29	Brewer's labourer
Cheetham Thomas	74	Publican & Brewer
Earp Thomas	30	Partner in Brewery employing 21 men
Fotherby T.	21	Brewer's labourer
Gadsby William	25	Brewer's drayman
Hewitt George	41	Brewer's traveller
Hutchinson Arthur	22	Brewer's labourer
Hooton James	38	Common brewer
Hopkin James		Brewer
Lanybain Thomas	39	Brewer's clerk
Payne James	31	Brewer
Parker John	45	Brewer's drayman
Pepper Thomas	27	Brewer
Pollard William	40	Brewer
Pollard William	16	Brewer
Pollard William	53	Brewer's Labourer
Rosell John	19	Brewery Clerk
Sharp William	55	Brewer
Sheppard	33	Brewer
Smith Jonas	58	Brewer
Smith Jonas	25	Brewer
Slater William	15	Brewer's clerk
Stevenson John	34	Brewer's labourer
Thompson Samuel	27	Brewer's labourer
Walton George	14	Brewer's servant
Walton Henry	28	Brewer & Hotel keeper
Walton Thomas	52	Brewer & Hotel keeper
Warwick Richard	42	Brewer & Banker clerk
Warwick Wm. D.	17	Clerk in Brewery
Warwick Samuel	29	Brewer's clerk
White Frederick	37	Brewer
Wright William	33	Brewer's labourer
Yeomans Thomas	55	Brewer

An analysis of particular occupations within the brewing trade as listed in the 1891 Census for Newark.

Occupation	Number	Occupation	Number
Labourers	69	Chemist	1
Clerks	34	Cashier	1
Brewers	12	Horse Keeper	1
Draymen	12	Number Taker	1
Coopers	7	Racksman	1
Travellers	7	Engineer	1
Bottlers	6	Engine driver	1
Foremen	4	Copperman	1
Cellarmen	2	Night watchman	1
Pupils	2	Fireman	1
Carters	2		

1.

2.

4.

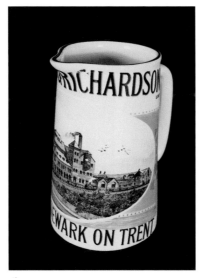

5.

3.

1. Facade of the Northgate Brewery today.

2. Coat of Arms on the Northgate offices.

3. Label commemorating an ale brewed for the wedding of Princess Elizabeth and The Duke of Edinburgh.

4. Commemorative Jug – Trent Brewery.

5. Commemorative Jug – Warwicks & Richardson's Brewery.

6. Advertising Poster

7. Northgate Maltings, built c.1860.

6.

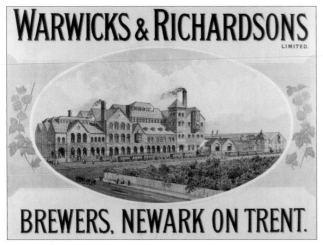

7.

Bottle Labels
from
Warwicks and Richardson's Northgate Brewery

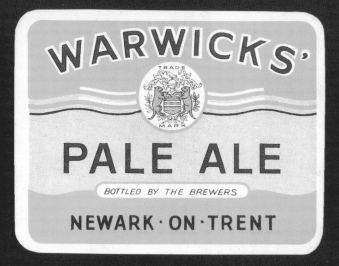

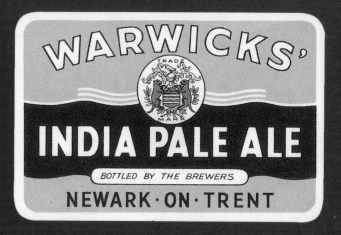

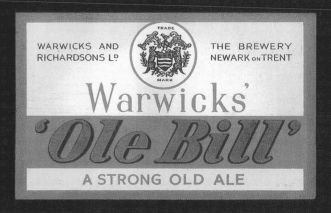

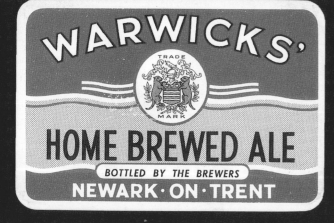

Workers at Warwicks & Richardson's Brewery, Northgate, pictured in the brewery yard. Second from the right William Pratt, cellarman.

Staff at James Hole & Co.'s Castle Brewery, c1914. Front row(seated) left to right: Harry Peet (in charge of cask cellars); Arthur Pass (brewery foreman); 'Old Man Tandy'(in charge of Shire horses and transport); a brewer; James Reynolds Hole (Director and son of James Hole Snr); Edward Kercheval Marsland – in riding habit – (managing director); James Hole Snr; A. Botsford (head brewer); Charles Henry Dixon (secretary and cashier); T. H. Heron (second brewer).
Standing on the extreme right of the photograph is Bill Tandy (bottling foreman later to become brewery foreman).
Among the others on the photograph are Dick Smalley; 'little' Brailsford (a brewery worker who also carried all the books and ledgers from the safe to the various departments each morning); 'Old Man' Pask (with a white beard and a white coat, third row from the back); W. Plummer; Tommy Trickett;

12. THE DECLINE OF THE BREWING INDUSTRY IN NEWARK

The peak of prosperity for brewers nationally was reached in the 1880s and 1890s. This is reflected in Newark's industry, the building of all the town's principal breweries - Warwicks & Richardson's, James Hole & Co. and Goodwins took place during this period.

After 1900, however, brewers everywhere complained of the distraction of their customers away from public houses. Consumers were becoming more ready to spend their declining wages on cheap, mass produced items for the home and packaged foodstuffs, rather than drink. Though real wages declined, expectations began to rise. Labourers were more ready to spend on their families and take a pride in their homes than simply to 'drown their sorrows' and drink away their meagre earnings. To this extent, at least, the vigorous Temperance Movements of the previous decades had had some success. There were now other leisure outlets - the music halls, cheap railway excursions and sporting fixtures - which could be enjoyed by all the family.

Dereliction in the barrel yard at Hole's Brewery, 1995.

In addition to this apparent change of attitude on the part of the public, brewers were also facing licensing restrictions brought in by W.E. Gladstone's Conservative government between 1869 and 1874, limiting the number of outlets. This led to competition between brewers, to acquire more tied houses. In national terms, the output from Britain's brewers fell by as much as 16% between 1876 and 1881.

The Liberal Government after 1906 increased the pressure on brewers with proposals to increase duty on public houses steeply. By 1914, it is said that over 90% of all licensed property had been bought by the brewers themselves. The value of licensed property rocketed (a list of Newark public houses and their owners may be found in Rodney Cousins' booklet 'Newark's Inns and Public Houses' - see bibliography).

Competition for outlets led to competition between the breweries themselves, with the period between 1895 and 1902 being dubbed 'The Brewers' Wars'. Many breweries became limited liability companies and issued large numbers of debenture and preference shares in order to raise capital to finance the acquisition of more tied houses, many at very high prices. Their profitability after 1900 was largely determined by the scale of their borrowing before that date. Many breweries had over-reached themselves in the 'glory days' and now found themselves with more capacity than they could utilise, with no way of raising money, in a contracting market, to pay off their debts. The result was that by 1914, the brewing industry became settled in the hands of a few companies who controlled almost the entire number of available licences.

During the First World War, the price of raw materials rose, as did duty. As a consequence, the price of beer rose sharply and production slumped. The brewers however, were to some extent cushioned from the full impact of the poor trading conditions by the reductions in the original gravities (on which duty had to be paid), most of which were ordered by the Central Control Board, as a contribution towards the War Effort. Lloyd George, during 1915, had blamed the shortage of munitions on brewers and the 'lure of drink' which he said was, "doing us more damage in the war than all the German submarines together". The brewing industry was threatened with nationalisation.

After the war, although consumption per head improved, it never regained pre-war levels. Developments in transport meanwhile, were ensuring that horse-drawn brewers' drays became a thing of the past with their place being taken by fleets of delivery lorries which were able to cover a far greater radius from their base. This facilitated the rationalisation of companies and enabled the remaining breweries to be fully utilised.

Warwicks & Richardson's, 1997. The barrel yard is deserted, but the brewhouse stands as a proud reminder of a vanished era. This picture makes an interesting comparison with that on page 24.

Between 1920 and 1930 the number of breweries nationally was more than halved. Other trends during this Inter-War period included the decline in the number of off-licences, but a massive increase in the number of registered drinking clubs (to over 18,000). This resulted in intense competition for the free-trade customers. There was an increase in expenditure in advertising and development of reciprocal trading agreements as 'national brands' developed. The 1930s saw an increase in the consumption of ale and bottled beer to a point where it more or less displaced the old-style porter. By 1938 bottled beer represented 25% of the market, eventually reaching 33% by 1950.

The Second World War, like the First, brought shortages of raw materials and this led to substitution of inferior materials and dilution of beer. Because there was a shortage of other consumer goods, however, consumption and output of beer rose. After 1945, demand fell back as other consumer goods became more available and production and selling costs rose. Demand continued to fall throughout the 1950s as brewers struggled to cope with high levels of duty and the need to renovate and improve their tied properties at high prices.

Between 1959 and 1963, truly national brewing firms were created by merger and acquisition, and six great conglomerates began to dominate the industry - Bass Charrington, Allied Breweries, Whitbread, Watney/Grand Metropolitan Hotels, Scottish & Newcastle and the Courage/Imperial Group. Together they accounted for 82% of UK beer sales. Emphasis was placed on speeding up the brewing process with the development of much larger production units. The improved road networks, meanwhile, enabled production facilities to be more heavily centralised.

Following the 1961 Licensing Act, brewers were able to take advantage of supermarket and increased off-licence sales (the number of off-licences increased by 64% between 1950 and 1980) and supply to food and leisure outlets. UK beer production reached a peak in 1979 when 40.5 million bulk barrels were produced (compared with 24.8 million in 1951). This was followed by a fall in 1980 and since then, production has run at about 10% less than the 1979 figures.

Growth in the export trade of UK beers has been largely prevented by the heavy cost of transport and the high rate of duty. The main development has been direct or indirect investment by British brewing companies in foreign businesses, for example in Belgium and the Netherlands. The majority of foreign lagers now sold in this country, are brewed by British firms under licence.

Although there has been a tendency towards enlarging companies, there is evidence that this has not necessarily made them more financially viable. 'Bigger' has not necessarily been 'better' and the national companies now tend to be regionally organised.

Another development has been a revival of interest in 'real ale' (*cask conditioned beer*) which, by the mid 1970s, represented 15% of the market. In Newark there have been various attempts to promote real ale in recent years, including the setting up of the West Crown Brewery in the

Peter Ward, Production Director at John Smith's Tadcaster Brewery (left), presenting Derick Warwick with a painting of his ancestor William Deeping Warwick, August 1988. The painting is by Frederick Yates, 1896.

The Courage Shire Horse team in Newark Market Place. From The Newark Advertiser, 9th June 1995

George Street Maltings by Norman and Alan Rutherford in 1977.

Newark's brewing industry has reflected national trends. As we have seen, Warwicks & Richardson's, who absorbed all but one of the Newark breweries, chiefly in the 19th Century, were themselves taken over by John Smith's Tadcaster Brewery Co. Ltd., in 1962. James Hole & Co. were taken over by Courage, Barclay and Simonds in 1968, and in 1970, the two groups (John Smith's and Courage) were themselves merged. The Courage Group were then taken over by Elders IXL, who are now trading as Foster's Brewing Group, though still popularly referred to as 'Courages'.

A recent assessment by Jane MacFarlane of the decline of the brewing and malting trades in Newark, has concluded that 'although traditionally the major industry in Newark has been lost, the effect on the economy has been minimal. Brewing was never a labour intensive industry and so there were no massive job losses. Also the gradual nature of the decline allowed those made redundant to be absorbed naturally into other industries within the town'.

Sherwood House, William Younger and Company Limited's premises on Jessop Way, Newark.

This is largely true. Although brewing was a source of much of the town's wealth in the 19th and early 20th Centuries, according to the 19th Century censuses, it did not employ a proportionately large number of the population. Consequently, as it gradually declined during the 20th Century, it did not result in widespread unemployment. Many felt that 'the end' had come in the 1940s when many people were made redundant from the malting industry, but many of these, with the brewers, were absorbed into engineering which was enjoying Britain's economic boom.

Although beer is no longer brewed in Newark, the town is still an important centre for sales and distribution. The latest development on the Newark brewing scene, has been the establishment of the new Courage Newark Business Unit in Jessop Way on the town's industrial estate. The new facility, known as Sherwood House, provides a full range of trade services to customers in an area spanning predominantly Lincolnshire and Nottinghamshire. The Courage Shire Horse Team marked the move from the Northgate premises by making a delivery to the Queen's Head in the Market Place on Tuesday 6th June 1995. By 1996, the Courage business was sold by the Foster's Brewing Group to Scottish and Newcastle plc and Courage Newark is now an integral part of William Younger and Company Limited, the Regional Trading Company covering the Midlands and East Anglia.

At the time of writing (1997), the fate of Newark's two largest brewery buildings is still being debated. The plan to use Hole's for housing accommodation has failed, though some of their land has been built on. Both Hole's and Warwicks & Richardson's have been the subject of supermarket plans and it is possible that part of Warwicks may now become an Arts Centre.

13. THE CONTRIBUTION OF MALTSTERS AND BREWERS TO THE TOWN

In common with many 19th Century entrepreneurs and self made men, Newark's maltsters and brewers became caught up in the wave of 'nouveau riche' philanthropy which characterised the latter part of the century. Alderman Thomas Earp, a former partner in the Trent Brewery, gave the land for the new Magnus Grammar School on Earp Avenue as well as contributing with J.G. Branston, the family of Sir William Gilstrap (maltsters) and James Hole to the foundation of the School of Science and Art (later to become the Lilley & Stone Girls' High School) on London Road.

The Maltsters, J.G. & H. Branston and James Hole & Co., all contributed significantly to the purchase of property on the south side of the Church where a number of run-down buildings needed to be removed to open up the view of the south porch and help protect the church from the danger of fire. J.G. Branston also purchased the old cattle market wharf and a house near Trent Bridge, from the Duke of Newcastle, to assist in provision of the Castle grounds as a pleasure garden for the town, whilst it was through the action of (Sir) William Gilstrap that the larger part of the gardens were created from the old Cattle Market. Sir William Gilstrap will always be remembered for his gift to the town in 1882-83 of the Free Library in Castlegate (now the Gilstrap Heritage Centre and Tourist Information Office).

The Magnus Grammar School, Earp Avenue.

Across Beastmarket Hill, meanwhile, one of Newark's most noted landmarks, the Ossington Coffee Palace, owes its existence to the reaction of Lady Ossington and the Temperance movement to the prevalence of 'the demon drink' in Newark. Interestingly, land for the Ossington was bought by Lady Ossington from the Handleys - the brewer-bankers.

In the old Newark Hospital on London Road, temperance and malting came together. The Ossington and Branston Wards were named after their benefactors and the building originally stood in a garden donated by Henry Branston and Alderman Becher Tidd Pratt, the latter having been seven times Mayor of Newark.

Finally, nearly a third of the stained glass windows which enhance Newark's medieval Parish Church were donated by maltsters and brewers and their families, and their monuments still adorn the Church's walls. The Church of St. Mary Magdalene provides a lasting memorial and resting place for this group of businessmen and philanthropists who dominated the town's commerce during the 19th and early 20th Centuries.

The contribution made to the town by brewers and maltsters

The School of Science and Art, London Road.

The Ossington Coffee Palace, Beastmarket Hill.

Newark Hospital, London Road.

The Castle Grounds (c.1890)

The space cleared on the south side of the church to create a fire break between the Market Place properties and the church.

The Gilstrap Free Library, Castlegate.

14. NEWARK'S NOTABLE BREWERS: BIOGRAPHIES

CAPARN, John Smith (1815-1890), was the eldest son of Richard and Mary Caparn. He was baptised at Newark Parish Church on 20th December 1815 and married Catherine Ann Betts in 1852 at Newark Parish Church and by her had five children. He was in partnership with John Wilson as a maltster in Lombard Street and lived in Carter Gate, and Castlegate and later at North Collingham. He was elected Mayor of Newark in 1853. He founded the Castle Brewery in Albert Street in partnership with Douglas Hankey. He died on 27th April 1890.

DAVY, Walter Shirley (1870-1949). A native of Ringwood, Hampshire, W.S. Davy took over the former Goodwins' Brewery on Balderton Gate in 1898. It was he who rechristened it the Devon Brewery, by which name it is best remembered. In later life Mr. Davy retired to Montague House at Retford, having been for many years a prominent and valued member of Newark Town Council. Between 1909 and 1913 he was Chairman of the Board of Governors of Newark Hospital and in 1918 he married Miss Harris who was then the Hospital Matron. Following the merger of the Devon Brewery with Warwicks & Richardson's, Mr Davy left Newark to become Chairman and Managing Director of Messrs. Truswells' Brewery at Sheffield. He attended his office at the brewery until the day before his death in April 1949.

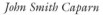

John Smith Caparn

EARP, Thomas (1830-1910), was the only son of William Earp of Derby, who had married Sarah the daughter of Mr. James Taylor of Muskham. Thomas was born in 1830 and educated at Derby Diocesan School. He became a maltster and brewer in Newark and a partner in Messrs. Earp & Slater's Trent Brewery. In 1874 he was returned as Liberal MP for Newark and again in 1880. He was also three times Mayor (1869, 1891, 1892) and a J.P. He died on 17th February 1910.

GOODWIN, John (c.1833-1896), was born at Braintree, Essex, as were his three eldest children, William, Ellen and Fleming. Gerald, the youngest, was born at Dunmow, Essex in 1867. John Goodwin moved to Newark with his wife, Elizabeth (born in Yorkshire) and family in the late 1870s and became managing partner in Caparn and Hankey & Co.'s Castle Brewery. Later he took over the Baldertongate Brewery which, after his death (on 24th November 1896), was managed by his two sons William and Fleming (Gerald entered holy orders).

Thomas Earp

HANDLEY, William (1746-1798), was the eldest son of William and Sarah Handley. He married Anne Marshall of Pickering and by her, had four sons - William Farnsworth, John, Benjamin and Charles Richard. He owned property in Castlegate, Northgate and elsewhere and was a partner, until 1791, in what became Pocklington and Dickinson's Bank. He was in partnership with Samuel Sketchley, Jessop and Marshall (his brother-in-law) in the Town Wharf Brewery and also in the Newark Cotton Mill, off Millgate, with Youle and Sketchley. Reporting his death in 1798, the Nottingham Journal said 'a friend of the poor, he was equalled by few, his big house being an asylum for the cries of the distressed'.

HANDLEY, William Farnsworth (1780-1851), was the eldest son of William and Ann Handley. He did not marry. He joined his late father's brewing business when he came of age in 1801 and was also a partner in the Newark New Bank until 1809. He was elected M.P. in 1831 and 1832 and retired in 1835. He was elected a Town Councillor in 1836. He was described as a 'good old English Gentleman who kept his hunters and a lot of servants in livery, which was claret cloth, crimson collars, cuffs and waistcoat, black velvet breeches; a butler, cook, kitchen maid, 3 house maids' (see 'The Handley Family of Newark and Sleaford' by Colonel R.C. Handley). He lived at Handley House on Northgate.

HANDLEY, John (1782-1856), was the second son of William and Ann Handley, born at Newark 20th March 1782. He married Martha, daughter of the Reverend Philip Storey of Locking Hall, Leicestershire. He became a partner with his brother, William Farnsworth Handley, in the family brewing firm. He lived at Muskham Grange and was a Town Councillor, also High Sheriff of Nottinghamshire in 1836.

*HEPPENSTALL, Christopher (1811-1872). Christopher Heppenstall, the son of a shoemaker, began work in the brewery trade in Sleaford, Lincolnshire. A man of initiative, by 1851 Christopher had established what he liked to call 'my brewery' – the 'Albion Brewery' in Newark employing a workforce of six men. He had also, in the same year, purchased four beerhouses, adding four more later. He owned other properties and bequeathed a dwelling in Baldertongate to his brother Frederick. Christopher became a churchwarden and member of the Grand Jury, Newark. Christopher and his wife Maria had no children of their own and, following his death in 1872, the Albion Brewery business was shared equally between two nephews, the cousins Christopher Heppenstall (b.1832) and the Reverend Frederick Heppenstall (b.1835). The Rev. Frederick died in 1879 and trustees managed his affairs thereafter.

*HEPPENSTALL, Christopher (1832-1886). Initially employed with the Inland Revenue, Christopher Heppenstall, the younger, qualified in 1853 as a surveyor of Brewers, Maltsters and Spirit Dealers. He became responsible for supervising 45 breweries and 8 Maltsters in the Beeston area of Nottinghamshire, before taking over a similar position at Louth in Lincolnshire. In 1872 be became joint owner of the Albion Brewery in Newark with his cousin, the Reverend Frederick Heppenstall. Shortly afterwards Frederick sold his half share of the brewery and Eagle Tavern to Christopher. Christopher became a Town Councillor and served on several committees, with the *Newark Advertiser* commenting on his "most benevolent disposition, and unfailing kindness to the poor". His son, Harold Wood Heppenstall, attended the school in Cambridge where the Reverend Frederick was Headmaster, whilst the latter maintained close ties with Newark through his shared ownership of property with Christopher.

James Hole

HERON, Thomas Henry (1874-1969). Born at Brandon, County Cork, Ireland, Thomas Heron came to London as a young man to study brewing with his uncle. He moved to Newark in 1902 and became second brewer at Hole's Castle Brewery. For many years he was a judge at the Brewers' Exhibition and Chairman of the Operative Brewers' Guild (Midland Section). He became Head Brewer for Hole's at the beginning of the First World War and retired in 1938. He was President of Newark Town and District Club and served as a sidesman at Newark Parish Church. He died on 1st February 1969.

HOLE, James (1827-1914), was descended from a family of maltsters based at Caunton Manor and became senior partner in the malting firm of Messrs. James Hole & Co., whose offices were on Northgate. In 1885, with Mr. S.K. Marsland (his first cousin once removed), he took over the Castle Brewery from Caparn, Hankey & Co. James Hole took an active part in town affairs and was twice Mayor (in 1888 and 1898). He was renowned for his 'unfailing courtesy, the charm and grace of his manner, and the unruffled urbanity of his disposition'. In public affairs he was valued for his 'shrewdness and foresight, a clear outlook, and a well-balanced judgement'. He lived with his wife (a Miss Esam of Averham) at Westfield House, Farndon (and their son Mr. J.R. Hole at The Homestead, Balderton). James Hole was an Alderman of Nottinghamshire County Council, a Governor of Newark Hospital, a Trustee of St. Leonard's Charity, the Magnus Charity and the School of Science and Art.

---

* The information on both Christopher Heppenstalls has been supplied by Mr B. W. Heppenstall, a descendant of the Heppenstall family of brewers.

HOOTON, James (1823-1875), was the son of William and Anne Hooton and was baptised at Newark Parish Church on 12th April 1823. His father, William, was also a brewer and James continued the tradition at the Oliver Cromwell Brewery, where he died on 3rd March 1875.

MARSLAND, Samuel Kercheval (1853-1900), was born on 28th December 1863, son of Rev. G. Marsland, Rector of Beckingham (his mother was the sister of Dean Hole of Rochester). He was educated at the Magnus Grammar School in Newark and Lancing College. On leaving school he joined James Hole (his first cousin once removed), in his malting business and subsequently moved with him to the Castle Brewery where he became a partner and Managing Director. He represented the East Ward on the Town Council and was elected Mayor in 1890 at the early age of 37. He became Chief Magistrate and was elected to the County Council in 1892. He was interested in Sport, especially football, and also the Volunteer movement. He was a worshipper at St Leonard's Church where he was also a Sidesman. He lived at Osmondthorpe House, Appletongate, before moving to Winthorpe with his wife (daughter of Rev. Edward Lamb, Vicar of Elmton,

Samuel Kercheval Marsland

Derbyshire) and their son, Edward Kercheval, who followed his father into the Castle Brewery business. He died 29th January 1900 and the funeral was held at Winthorpe Church.

MOSS, William (*c*.1824-1892). Born the son of a Newark saddler, Moss served his apprenticeship in the printing business of John Wells, Barnby Gate, marrying his eldest daughter. Following the death of Mr. Wells in *c*.1855, Moss took over the printing business and subsequently became involved in furniture auctioneering. Liberal in outlook, Moss became the first publisher of the reconstituted *Newark Herald* newspaper in 1872, although he quickly found that his political views alienated him from many of his influential friends and acquaintances. He withdrew from the *Herald* in 1874. He subsequently stood for election as a Town Councillor (unsuccessfully) but was created an Alderman when the Liberals gained power in the town. He continued in the printing and furnishing trade on Barnby Gate until 'Moss Auction Mart' was acquired by Messrs. Goodwin Bros. for their brewery. In 1884 Moss himself acquired the Cromwell Brewery in Barnby Gate, selling it sometime before 1889 to L.C. Barstow & Co.

Joseph Richardson

RICHARDSON, Joseph (1825-1894), became a partner in Marfleet's malting business in Northgate, then senior partner of Messrs. Richardson, Earp and Slater of the Trent Brewery, Millgate. When that business was amalgamated with Richard Warwick and Sons, Mr Richardson became a Director of Messrs. Warwicks & Richard-son's Ltd. He was twice elected as a Town Councillor and served as Mayor in 1881.

Samuel Sketchley's Memorial in St. Mary Magdalene Church.

SKETCHLEY, Samuel (*c*.1741-1831), was the eldest of eight children of Samuel and Elizabeth Sketchley of Burton-on-Trent, and was baptised on 11th November 1741. He married Elizabeth Ley there on 6th April 1763. He arrived in Newark about 1766, leased the Town Wharf Brewery from the Duke of Newcastle and went into partnership with the Handleys. He was Senior Alderman of the Borough for many years, and Mayor in 1791 and 1804. He lived in a house overlooking Trent Bridge, now (1997) Holden's furniture store. Elizabeth Sketchley died in 1808 and Samuel on 31st December 1831. He was buried on 5th January 1832 and both are commemorated by inscriptions in the south transept of the Parish Church. An obituary in the *Nottingham and Newark Mercury* recorded that Samuel, was the oldest inhabitant of the town.

Samuel does not appear to have had any children but was survived by a nephew, also called Samuel, who married Jane Jemima Forster (daughter of Richard and Helen Forster) 22nd January 1814. Their son Richard Forster Sketchley (baptised 25th July 1826) was a poet and local historian who became assistant keeper of the Science and Art Department at the South Kensington Museum in London, a post he held for 30 years.

An advertisement for Samuel Taylor's brewery at the Royal Oak on Stodman Street, 1865

SLATER, William (*c*.1830-1895). Slater is first listed as running the posting business at the Clinton Arms Inn in the Market Place, later moving next door to the Saracen's Head with his son, Henry. He became a partner in the Trent Brewery with Richardson and Earp. He had no taste for public life, but served the town for 20 years as a member of the Newark Board of Guardians, Overseer of the Poor and Church Warden.

TAYLOR, Samuel (1822-1865), the son of William and Mary Taylor (née Porter) was baptised at Newark on 1st August 1822. He is listed as a Maltster in 1839 and lived at the Royal Oak Inn in Stodman Street, which like many public houses, had a small brewhouse. He died after a protracted illness at the early age of 42 on 10th April 1865 and was described in his obituary as a 'brewer, wine and spirit merchant' of Stodman Street. His wife, Elizabeth (born at Kingston, Surrey *c*.1822) continued the business until her death on 3rd April 1874, aged 52, when it was taken over by Samuel (the second of her four children).

WARWICK, William (1794-1838), was the son of Richard Warwick and Sarah (née Bailey) of Lockton, Yorkshire. William Warwick was born at Pickering on 1st February 1794, coming to Newark in about 1809 as a clerk in Handley & Co.'s bank. On 13th May 1816 he married Mary, daughter of William Deeping of Hawton, at Southwell Minster. They had six sons and six daughters, and a residence on Northgate. William Warwick died on 29th April 1838 at Newark and was buried at Hawton after serving for 29 years with Handley's bank. It was William's second son, Richard, who became head of Handley's brewery.

WARWICK, Richard (1818-1877), was the second son of William and Mary Warwick (see above). He was born at Newark on 8th September 1818 and baptised in the Parish Church the following day. In March 1842 he married Sarah Robinson of Bulcote in Nottinghamshire, by whom he had five children: William

Richard Warwick

Deeping, Richard Huskinson, Emily, John Francis and Kate.

Richard became manager first of Smith's Bank in the Market Place, and latterly of William Handley's Town Wharf Brewery which he bought in 1856. Richard subsequently established his own brewery in Northgate and took his three sons into partnership He became Mayor in 1868 and was also a Church Warden and Overseer of the Poor. He died on 12th March 1877.

WARWICK, William Deeping (1843-1913), was the eldest son of Richard and Sarah Warwick (see above), born on 30 July 1843. He married Emily Sarah, eldest surviving daughter of Henry Branston of Newark, a noted local maltster. They took up residence at Balderton Hall (subsequently incorporated into Balderton Hospital) and had five children - three sons and two daughters. Following his father's death in 1877, William Deeping became senior partner in the family brewing firm.

William Deeping Warwick

WARWICK, Richard Huskinson (1849-1909), the second son of Richard and Sarah Warwick, was born at Newark on 30th April 1849. On 20th September 1877 he married Florence Mary, third surviving daughter of Henry Branston, a noted local maltster. Together they had five children, two sons and three daughters. Their home was at Easthorpe, Southwell. Richard's wife died at Burgage Manor, Southwell, on 21st January 1888. Richard subsequently married again, this time in Edinburgh to Clara Percy Combe, daughter of Chas. Thompson Combe of Clarendon Crescent, Edinburgh. They had one son, Norman Richard Combe, who was born on 5th October 1892 at Southwell. Clara died on 26th February 1899. Richard Huskinson Warwick joined his father and elder brother in the family brewing business in 1870. He died at Burgage Manor, Southwell, on 2nd October 1909.

WARWICK, John Francis (1854-1935). The youngest son of Richard and Sarah Warwick, John Francis was born on 2nd August 1854 at Newark. He married Eliza Gertrude, youngest daughter of Henry Branston, a noted local maltster. They had six children, four boys and two girls. Their home was at No. 1 South Parade off London Road in Newark, later moving to Upton Hall. John Francis was an active member in the family brewing firm for many years. Eliza Gertrude died on 6th April 1932, John Francis himself following her on 8th March 1935.

Richard Huskinson Warwick

WHITE, William (*c.*1809-1869), was born at Morton, Nottinghamshire, *c.*1809 and operated the Royal Oak Brewery in Castlegate before moving to a new brewery in Baldertongate in 1862. After his death in 1869, his wife, Dinah, moved back to the Royal Oak and continued the bottling business there. In 1888 she bought both the Royal Oak and the Ram Hotel next door, in the Duke of Newcastle's property sale. Dinah had been born at Milford, Derbyshire according to the 1881 census (though her obituary states she was born at Smockington, Leicester and the 1861 census suggests Claybrooke in Warwickshire). She was in business in Newark for 52 years, latterly with her son, George. She died on 1st May 1896, in her 78th year.

15. GLOSSARY

BACK	brewing term for a vessel.
BARREL	36 gallon cask.
BEER	originally a term used for a fermented drink made with malted barley and hops. The term is now used more loosely to include ales and lagers.
BITTER	pale or amber beer made with hops to give a bitter flavour.
BREWERY CONDITIONED	beer brought to perfect condition in the brewery, instead of maturing in cask or bottle.
BURTONISATION	water treated with minerals to make it similar to that found naturally at Burton-on-Trent.
CARAMEL	sugar treated with heat to give added colour to the beer.
CASK	beer container made of metal, formerly of wood.
CASK CONDITIONED BEER	beer matured in casks rather than in tanks in the brewery.
COMMON BREWER	a brewer who brewed for 'public' use (i.e. for more than his own institution) rather than 'private' use, .
COOPER	a maker and repairer of wooden casks.
COPPER	copper or stainless steel vessel used for boiling the wort to give its bitter flavour.
DRAUGHT	beer delivered through a tap.
FERMENTATION	the process by which beer is produced from wort by yeast.
FIRKIN	9 gallon cask.
GRAVITY	the measure of the density of liquids.
GRIST	crushed malt.
GYLE	fermenting wort.
HOGSHEAD	54 gallon cask.
HOPS	a perennial plant the flowers of which are used to give beer its bitter flavour.
HOP BACK	vessel used to remove the hops from boiled wort.
HOP POCKET	the sack used to deliver hops to the brewery.
ISINGLASS	semi-transparent substance obtained from the swim bladders of sturgeon, used to make beer clear.
KILDERKIN	18 gallon cask.
LAGER	light coloured beer of continental origin.
LAUTER TUN	vessel for filtering the mash.
LIQUOR	the brewer's term for water.
MALT	barley, steeped in water, allowed to germinate then heat treated to stop this.
MASHING	mixing together of grist and hot water to form malt sugars which will be fermented with yeast.
PALE ALE	beer brewed from pale malt, East India Pale Ale was first brewed for the Indian market.
PIN	$4\frac{1}{2}$ gallon cask.
PORTER	bitter beer, dark brown in colour, brewed from charred malt, named after the porters of the great London markets who first made it popular. Originally a mix of three beers, probably invented by Ralph Harwood of the Bell Brewery, Shoreditch, and called 'Entire Butt' or 'Harwood's Entire'!
RACKING	filling casks with beer.
SMALL BEER	weak beer.
SPARGING	spraying hot water over mash to ensure complete extraction of malt sugars.
TIPPLER	ale house keeper.
TUN	cask or fermenting vat.
VICTUALLER	one who has a licence to sell food and drink.
WORT	unfermented beer.
YEAST	a single celled micro-organism which causes fermentation.

16. APPENDICES

Appendix I Memories . . .

From before the Second World War, called to mind by Mr. Jack Walker of Hole's Brewery.

I remember . . .

Having to work in iron-shod clogs and the difficulty of climbing the iron stairs . . .

Working overtime scouring the refrigeration system with sand and water - the copper became black and purple from the hot beer . . .

Cleaning floors with caustic soda . . .

Bottling Guinness stripped to the waist because the Guinness was very sticky . . .

Men collecting their ration of beer from the cellar in mashing tins . . .

Seeing the last horse-drawn dray which was kept for local deliveries . . .

During the War - being brought fruit by the lorry drivers on the country runs . . .

Being paid in numbered metal tins (not wage packets) . . .

The good camaraderie - there was lots of fun as well as fights!

Training at the Fire Station for the fire watching at the brewery - free fish and chips were provided . . .

Mr Jack Walker today.

From the 1950s and 60s, called to mind by Norman and Margaret Powers of the bottling and mineral departments of Warwicks & Richardson's Brewery.

We remember . . .

Using caustic soda to remove labels and clean bottles . . .

Working from 7.30 am to 9.00 pm especially in hot summers when demand for beer and minerals was high . . .

Seeing the blacksmith making pub signs, the cooper making and repairing barrels, and the carpenter making furniture for pubs . . .

Finding the bottles of lemonade frozen solid and many smashed during the cold winter of 1963 . . .

Attending works' parties at the Town Hall . . .

Going up the old tower and seeing the siren (a relic of the Second World War) marked 'raiders approaching' and 'raiders passed' . . .

Norman and Margaret Powers today.

Making a 'den' in the middle of the pile of wooden cases in the cellars so that the girls could play cards in secret......

Enjoying Friday - the 'fun days' - when once the cleaning-up was done, there was no more work until 'clocking off time'.

Appendix II
Richard Warwick's Instructions for Brewing Malt Liquor

'Malt should be pale, plump, tender & sweet, well dried, crushed & ground. Some malt makers diminish the strength or saccharine quality of malt to obtain additional quantity, which is a bad practice & the maltsters at Ware & the neighbourhood have a high reputation by avoiding it. The most acute maltsters in Notts. are gradually adopting the Ware system & as the article will fetch a higher price in proportion, eventual success & general adoption is certain.

Hops should be ripe & full grown, strong yet pleasant & bitter, between yellow & green, clammy to the hand when pressed. Avoid brown hops. For private breweries some tops & copperbacks to the boilers, pressing of the hops after draining and machines for stirring the malt when mashing are not recommended. When a perforated interior moveable bottom is used in the mash tub (as a preferable drainer to a stroom) a space of about an inch is left from the bottom of the tub. It is advisable to have a perforated pipe of suitable diameter attached to the interior bottom & to rise above the mash within which another pipe without holes should slide down to the loose bottom & have a funnel top to receive the hot water for the mashing & conduct it to the space between the two bottoms from whence it will rise upwards among the malt & be diffused generally at the same time raising the grain and moisening it. If by accident in applying the water too hot; or by mixing ground barley amongst malt; or any other cause, the mash should settle to the bottom, through which the sweet Wort cannot pass; in that state it will be expedient to draw out the funnel and water pipe and allow the pipe with holes to strain & convey the wort to the bottom.

First Mash. If this plan is adopted the grain is to be first put into the mash tub and the water added at 160 degrees of heat by Fahrenheit, lower rather than higher about ten & a half gallons to every bushel of malt.

If not convenient to conduct the water as described the water is turned into the mash tub and when at 130 degrees the malt is added. In either case stir or rouse the malt i.e. the mash for 15 or 20 minutes. If malt only is mashed, let it stand one hour; but if ground barley is mixed therewith it will be necessary for the mash to stand three hours to allow of a saccharification to take place of the unmalted grain & what is effected by mixing with the malt. About six gallons of wort should run off per bushel, the other 4½ gallons (excepting the small quantity that has been evaporated) being taken up by saturation of the malt. Clear the barrels during the time the mashes are standing. If there are two coppers, be ready to pump the first wort from the gathering tub into the copper as soon as the second mash is laid on, and the copper ready to receive it. The overplus hot water may be removed from the large to the small copper if convenient to be ready for the third mash with which sufficient water may be heating preparatory to the second mash's being run off.

Second mash. Turn into the mash tub about four gallons of water per bushel at 180 degrees which it is unnecessary to rouse or disturb. Let it remain one hour, run off in the most convenient manner to get it into the copper quickly. The two run-offs will produce about ten and a half gallons per bushel. Boil the ale wort rapidly 45-60 minutes.

Small Beer
Third Mash. Put about five gallons of water to the bushel at any temperature from 175-185 degrees. Stir for about 15 minutes, and after running that off, if not inconvenient, pass through the grain a fourth mash of about five gallons to eight bushels at the same heat and let it stand and halt an hour. Boil the small beer rapidly for three quarters of an hour.

The latter mashes will yield nearly as much in wort as the quantity of water turned into the mash tub as the malt is saturated by the first mash.

The full advantage derived from the operation of boiling the worts is obtained as soon as the appearance of the liquor is changed to a broken and flaky state: and when kept in full ebullition the separation frequently takes place within ten minutes. This may be distinguished by taking a little of the wort in the hand bowl and inspecting it aside from the steam of the copper. Boiling a long time may do injury, and though, rather in conformity to the old custom, I have directed this process to be continued about an hour, I know from experience that one third of that time is sufficient.

It is material in the next stage of proceeding to cool the wort as quick as possible; of course an exposure to a stream of cold air and being spread thin is desirable. In large concerns besides having coolers in which the wort is less than 2 inches deep, they have canvass sails, wafting to and fro; and revolving canvass fliers, or fans, to increase the current and these are clearly great improvements in warm weather especially. Avoid washing tubs and soapy vessels; also be careful not to mix worts which are much different in their temperatures when cooling. Any part of the wort (if cooled in sundry vessels) may be 'put to barm' in the fermenting tub as soon as sufficiently cool, and the other parts added as they become fit. Many brewers keep out a quantity of the wort by way of regulating and exciting the vat during the time it is in the fermenting tub, but it is better to let it all ferment together equally, because every addition of the wort has to undergo the entire process and must therefore retard the completion of the vinous fermentation, and possibly may lead to the acetous. The modern term for this part of the process which of all others is the most important is attenuation, as in the course of working, or fermenting the specific gravity becomes less; and by observing the diminution by the saccharometer you are able to ascertain when the liquor is sufficiently thinned, or attenuated, in other words, when the fermentation is perfect. Attenuation is considerably more active in warm weather than in cold; windy weather also accelerates, and extremely cold weather retards fermentation.

When the vat is found to be too cold it is advisable to fill a cask or tin vessel with a long neck to rise out of the vat, with hot water; let either (of size suitable to the quantity of *gyle*) into the fermenting vessel. On the contrary if the vat be too hot a quantity of cold water may be immersed in the same manner. Try the heat by the thermometer and the strength by the saccharometer frequently; and register the changes in your Journal

Table during the course of the fermentation.

Mr Tuck says 'the diminution is about one half of the previous weight'.

Ale required for use at an early age should be fermented a few degrees warmer than when intended for keeping; it will ripen and fine sooner and will be fit for drinking in small casks earlier than in large ones. If the vat be uncontrollably warm in the tub and the head assumes a dark & spotted appearance; it is advisable to separate and check the fermentation by tunning, for if not subdued, it would probably lead to the acetous fermentation, however there is no danger in moderate quantities if kept below 80 degrees though that is higher than is requisite.

On the contrary a cold and languid vat must have the temperature raised by closing the windows, and door, by covering over the fermenting tub or by a sprinkling of flour & salt; or by immersing a cask or other vessel filled with hot water. The head may appear delicately beautiful and pleasing to the eye, and yet from coldness the operation may not be complete, and a dangerous fermentation will probably occur after the ale has been some time in the barrels; nor will the liquor be fine or palatable until the fermentation is perfected. It is said that fermentation will begin at as low a temperature as 50 degrees but of this I have had no experience.

Fining. The Isinglass as bought at druggists' and grocers' is made without heat from the bladders of sturgeons, chiefly near the Caspian Sea. An inferior sort is made from the tails etc. of the same fish. In many large breweries the dried skins of the Soles are now substituted. One pound of good Isinglass will make 12 gallons of finings, thus, Bruise it and pull it into pieces and put it into a tub with as much common vinegar as will cover it, or sour beer will do for the purpose; in this the Isinglass will swell and dissolve & mild beer may be used to thin it with. Agitate it frequently with a stiff whisk; with which also urge it through a hair sieve or it may be strained through a coarse linen bag, into another tub by pressure. From a pint to a quart will be necessary for a barrel according to the state of the ale to be purified and this should be diluted with a quantity of the beer to be cleared, whisking it till it froths, then pour it into the cask, stirring briskly and bung close. This mixture may be tried first in half a pint of liquor in a bottle, take half a teaspoonful of the preparation and shake them together, then let the bottle remain still. The cloudiness will soon collect into flakes and settle to the bottom, unless the fermentation should be incomplete and in that case the clearing will not be so perfect and of course it would be the same in the cask if the beer is disturbed by renewed fermentation and 'on the fret'. To dissolve the Isinglass by heat would destroy the clarifying property.

Copied August 2nd (18)55
(The preceding instructions for brewing were first written by Mr Tho. Wilson of Newark.)

Appendix III
A list of Sixteenth Century brewers and tipplers (alehouse keepers) from the Quarter Session Records

Baldertongate

Ch(arles) Handley	bruer
Robert Storr	bruer
Mrs Meringe	bruer
Wife Taylor	bruer
John Machin	bruer
Wife Parrishe	bruer
Stephane Tyborow	tipler
Henry Barret	tipler
Wife Chapman	tipler
Richard Homes	tipler
Wife Wilkinson	tipler

Barnebygate

Richard Backhouse	bruer
William Coolinge	bruer
William Richardson	tipler
Wife Willes	tipler

Appletongate

Edwarde Walker	bruer
George Croppe	bruer
John Pacey	bruer
Robert Awood	tipler
Thomas Scott	tipler

17. SELECT BIBLIOGRAPHY

BARNARD, Alfred. *The Noted Breweries of Great Britain and Ireland*, Causton & Sons, 1889-91

BREWERS Guardian, Centenary Issue, 1971

BROWN, Cornelius. *A History of Newark-on-Trent*, S. Whiles 1904-07 (two volumes)

CLARK, Peter. *The English Ale House: A Social History 1200-1830*, Longmans, 1983

COUSINS, P.R. *Newark's Inns and Public Houses*, Nottinghamshire County Council, 1991

HANDLEY, Colonel R.C. *The Handley Family of Newark and Sleaford*

HEMINGWAY, G.Y. *The Caparn Family of Newark and Some of Their Descendants*, unpublished typescript, 1979

HEMINGWAY, G.Y. *The Handley Family*, Unpublished typescript.

JAMES HOLE & CO. LTD., *Hole's Newark Ales*, James Hole & Co. Ltd., c.1935

LOVETT, Maurice. *Brewing and Breweries*, Shire Publications

MACFARLANE, Jane. *The Decline of the Brewing and Malting Industries in Newark-upon-Trent and its Effect Upon the Re-Structuring of Industry in the Town*, unpublished BA Dissertation, Leeds University 1992.

MATHIAS, Peter. *The Brewing Industry in England 1700-1830*, Cambridge University Press

STEPHENS, Peter (ed.) *Newark: The Magic of Malt*, Nottinghamshire County Council, 1993

TURTON, Richmond (ed.) *The Brewing Industry: A Guide to Historical Records*, Manchester University Press, 1990.

18. INDEX

*Signature of Samuel Sketchley, 'father' of
Newark's brewing industry.*

© Brenda M. Pask 1997

ISBN 0 902751 18 2

Published jointly by Nottinghamshire County Council and Newark & Sherwood District Council, and sponsored by William Younger and Company Limited.

Typeset in 11.5/12 Galliard
and Printed by Central Print Services, Nottinghamshire County Council